To

Garner Anthony,

With best

wishes,

Henry Kaufman

6/19/86

INTEREST RATES,
THE MARKETS,
AND THE
NEW FINANCIAL
WORLD

Interest Rates, the Markets, and the New Financial World

Henry Kaufman

Times BOOKS

Copyright © 1986 by Salomon Brothers, Inc.
All rights reserved under International and Pan-American
Copyright Conventions. Published in the United States by Times
Books, a division of Random House, Inc., New York, and
simultaneously in Canada by Random House of Canada Limited,
Toronto.

Book design by The Sarabande Press

Library of Congress Cataloging-in-Publication Data
Kaufman, Henry.
Interest rates, the markets, and the new financial world.
Bibliography: p.
Includes index.
1. Finance.
2. International finance.
3. Capital market.
4. Interest rates.
I. Title.
HG173.K364   1986   332   86–5865
ISBN 0–8129–1333–7

Manufactured in the United States of America

9   8   7   6   5   4   3   2

First Edition

To Charles Simon
with affection and appreciation

ACKNOWLEDGMENTS

We all benefit from others and very little of what we do is ultimately our very own. And so it is with this book. To be sure, I wrote it but I benefited from many. The insights I gleaned from my early business experience and from my nearly twenty-five years of work at Salomon Brothers were the result of many discussions with talented people, some of whom will be acknowledged in a later chapter. Suffice it to say that for the thoughts and ideas that have gone into this book, I was at the right place at the right time.

In the preparation of the statistical information as well as in checking the accuracy of many of the statements made in the book, I have been aided by some of our gifted research personnel. I am indebted to: Richard Berner, Steven Blitz, Barbara Cannon-Jones, Robert V. DiClemente, Oliver D'Oelsnitz, Michael Fung, Aaron S. Gurwitz, Jeffrey Hanna, Susan M. Hering, Richard I. Johannesen, Jr., Nancy Kimelman, Judy Lewis, John Lipsky, James McKeon, Jerry Pegden, Kenneth T. Rosen, and Nicholas Sargen.

I am grateful to Mel Adams and Charles Brophy, who provided me with counsel and comments that helped focus on this book.

I am also grateful for the dedication and devotion of my secretary, Helen Katcher, and of Margaret O'Neill, in helping me to complete this work.

I am especially indebted to Professor Lawrence S. Ritter, of the Graduate School of Business Administration of New York University. His meticulous editing and many helpful suggestions were invaluable in the preparation of the text.

CONTENTS

Contents

III. INTEREST RATES

Contents

PART I

Introduction

CHAPTER 1

From Wenings to Wall Street

When I joined Salomon Brothers in January 1962, financial life proceeded at a tranquil and leisurely pace. Interest rates were not the focus of national attention the way they are today, and the head of the Federal Reserve, William McChesney Martin, Jr., was hardly the household name Paul Volcker has become.

The daily flow of financial transactions ran along traditional lines. Corporations issued long-term bonds and satisfied their short-term money needs mostly by borrowing from commercial banks. The U.S. Government was only slightly in deficit, and financial institutions knew who they were and what they were supposed to be doing. Banks accepted deposits and made loans, insurance companies provided insurance coverage, brokerage houses bought stocks and bonds, and no one strayed into anyone else's territory.

A modest band of institutional investors pursued fixed-rate investments using rather simple analytical techniques. Bond and stock investors each went their own way. Only a handful of Wall Streeters tracked the daily and weekly operations of the Federal Reserve and the U.S. Treasury, and fluctuations in the money supply (the Federal Reserve published only one money supply number then, not three the way it does today) were followed by few academicians and virtually no practitioners.

To be sure, much academic work had been done on interest-rate theory over the years, including the writings of Irving Fisher, John Maynard Keynes, and Frederick R. Macaulay. And in 1962 Sidney Homer, my mentor and partner at Salomon Brothers, was putting the finishing touches on his monumental *A History of Interest Rates,* which would appear the following year. Nevertheless, in those days there was remarkably little interaction between academicians and financial practitioners.

In 1962 the ebb and flow of financial transactions produced yields that fluctuated in the range of 2½ to 3 percent for three-month Treasury bills and 4 to 4¼ percent for twenty-year Government bonds, while the prime loan rate charged by banks remained unchanged during that year at 4½ percent. Compare those yields with 17⅛ percent on bills, 15¼ percent on long-term Governments, and a 21½ percent prime rate in 1981. While interest rates have retreated from their 1981 peaks, they are still at levels today that would have been unthinkable only twenty years ago.

We have become sensitized not only by greater changes in interest rates but also by business developments, new financial practices and attitudes, and by governmental policy responses, all of which have combined from time to time to produce credit crunches and financial crises that conventional market wisdom did not anticipate. The first such crunch materialized in the summer of 1966, when the prime rate hit 6 percent, a high considered comparable to Mount Everest at the time. I vividly recall the fears and tensions that gripped the market then, sparked by an onslaught of deposit withdrawals that gave birth to the expression "financial disintermediation."

Subsequent financial upheavals included not only periodic bursts of financial disintermediation but also prominent failures and near bankruptcies, such as Penn Central (1970), Lockheed (1971), Franklin National Bank and Herrstatt (1973–74), W. T. Grant (1975), Chrysler (1979), Penn Square Bank (1982), and Continental Illinois (1984).

Today the focus on financial markets is intense. The placid days of yesteryear are gone, replaced by turbulence and volatility. Bond investors now generally resort to a complex matrix of risk-and-reward analysis encompassing investment opportunities abroad as well as at home. The monitoring and evaluating of Federal Reserve operations are now carried on by a virtual army of full-time professionals who labor to unearth the slightest monetary nuance. Markets react violently when the weekly monetary data differs too much from general expectations.

Chief financial officers more often than not are now members of the corporation's board of directors. In the corporate world, access to funds and terms of financing have become as important as marketing and production. Households similarly search out alternative borrowing and investing opportunities; their level of financial sophistication has improved markedly.

I have had the opportunity to spend a large portion of my professional life during these years of drastic change in financial behavior. Improved financial sophistication is of course all for the better, but many aspects of the changes that have taken place in financial behavior endanger our economy and perhaps even our political way of life unless those new practices are curbed.

Hence this book deals with the changes in financial behavior that have evolved in recent years, their implications, and what should be done about them. It ranges from financial markets to

5

the practices of financial institutions, from the growth of domestic debt to the complexities of the international debt problem, from budget deficits to monetary policy-making.

In the analyses and comments that follow, I have tried hard to be objective and impartial. But people are not robots, and economics and finance are hardly exact sciences; the way we react to economic developments depends partly on how life has shaped and molded us. So I don't think it inappropriate to comment briefly on people and events that have had an influence on my thinking, especially since some of the financial observations and opinions in this book, for better or worse, depart somewhat from the canons that seem to dominate economic thinking nowadays.

I suspect that my strong anti-inflation views had their genesis in my childhood. I was born in 1927 in Wenings, a small town in Germany, just in the aftermath of the hyperinflation. For many years in my early childhood and even after we fled Nazi persecution and came to the United States, I heard my grandfather's oft-repeated stories of how hyperinflation had destroyed financial values.

His own wealth totaled close to 200,000 deutsche marks after World War I and was mostly in savings accounts and investments in mortgages on land he had sold to others. All of it became worthless. This was not a singular tale but one that could be multiplied many times over in the tales of people who had spent a lifetime painstakingly building a nest egg for their old age, only to see it all vanish in just a couple of years.

This hyperinflation surely uprooted the values and morality of the middle class, the essential group in a democratic society, which in Germany was not deeply embedded to begin with. It contributed to a nationalistic class struggle in which Jews became the scapegoats in what had at one time seemed to be an enlightened and advanced society. Our democratic roots in the

United States are of course more deeply embedded. Nevertheless, we should not encourage national policies that push our economy to extremes, which would harm the well-being of our large middle class.

Only through policies that encourage noninflationary growth can we preserve one of the unique features of our country—the opportunity to succeed. I am a product of that American opportunity, which I hardly envisioned when I touched these shores as a ten-year-old in 1937. My father became a laborer, working twelve hours a day, six days a week. My mother did housework to earn money, working outside the home for the first time in her life. I was fortunate to have grandparents to take care of me when I came home from school.

Nor was this a singular experience. It occurred in an environment where effort, persistence, and merit were recognized. Few native-born Americans can fully appreciate the many positive distinctive characteristics of our way of life as much as can those who came here from elsewhere. To abuse our financial system, as we have done occasionally in recent decades, is to run the risk of changing for the worse our economic life-style, of ending the opportunity for individuals to advance in the class structure, and of threatening the heart of our political system.

How we conduct ourselves financially and how our financial institutions are motivated has much to do with our economic well-being. This is why I have strong views on how our financial system should be structured and how financial behavior should be disciplined; my occasional warnings are aimed at arresting trends that may tilt us in difficult-to-reverse directions.

My views have also been influenced by the stages of my professional career, first commercial banking, then central banking, and finally investment banking. When I received my master's degree from Columbia University in 1949, I went to work in the credit department of People's Industrial Bank in New York City, which later was acquired by Manufacturers Trust Company. This experience gave me an early insight into the cutting edge of banking practices that in later years became acceptable and were promoted by the larger commercial banks.

Just to mention a few, these practices included consumer credit, accounts-receivable financing, field warehousing arrangements, industrial equipment financing, and secured and unsecured lending to finance companies. Several impressions from this work have stayed with me, among them the realization that judgments on credits are not constant; they often vary with credit availability and the stage of the business cycle. The evaluation of credit risk and lender reward is far from an exact science.

I also learned fairly early that financial statements by themselves rarely provide a correct picture. They are subject to accounting rules and regulatory conventions, and at times are influenced in their preparation by senior management wanting to paint a happy picture. This applies to business as well as financial institutions. My work in the credit department taught me to question the extent to which outside analysts can obtain an intimate look at financial institutions—or nonfinancial institutions, for that matter; the information analysts obtain is heavily dependent on the veracity of the views expressed by the management of these institutions.

For example, I remember visiting a container company where People's Industrial Bank had a large loan collateralized by a field warehousing agreement. My job was to inspect the field warehousing setup. Field warehousing is an arrangement in which part of the borrower's premises is set aside as a place to keep the collateral that secures the loan. That part of the premises is called a field warehouse. An employee of the borrower is bonded with respect to that area, and the collateral can be moved in and out under certain conditions.

When I arrived at the borrower's place of business in Brooklyn, I found big containers of paper. Those that were in the factory were brand-new, but those in the field warehouse were old and damaged. In my report I wrote, "We don't have adequate collateral on this loan. We are significantly undercollateralized because nothing very good is in that field warehouse." The only way to learn that was to be there, at the factory; on paper everything looked just fine.

My experiences at the Federal Reserve Bank of New York, which I joined in 1957 as an economist when I was about to complete my doctorate at the Graduate School of Business Administration of New York University, added another dimension. I gained an appreciation of the awesome power of modern-day central banking to influence economic activity—although it was clear to me then, as it still is now, that central banking has its limitations. Its efficacy depends greatly on the talent and dedication of the central bankers themselves. Then and now, the Federal Reserve has been blessed with many exceptional people. Working on a daily basis with them for over four years helped to greatly expand my knowledge and understanding of financial matters.

I also sensed then and even now that the Federal Reserve asserts its power with deference and at times quite timidly, in recognition perhaps of the fact that it is only quasi-autonomous and that even the strongest of Fed leadership is encumbered by a bureaucracy. My stay at the Fed reinforced my early belief in the importance of *credit* as a policy variable, but it was later, after I joined Salomon Brothers, that I became convinced that although money matters, it is credit that counts.

My stay at the Fed, from mid-1957 through the end of 1961, encompassed a rather calm period of economic and financial behavior. There were two mild recessions, in 1958 and 1960. The most exciting interest-rate development occurred in 1959, when the U.S. Treasury issued the then-famous "Magic 5s," notes due in five years with a 5 percent coupon. The notes attracted substantial purchases by individuals. In those days, American stabilization policies would not tolerate inflation above 2 percent or so.

When I joined Salomon Brothers, in January 1962, the move

coincided with the start of a period in which financial markets were transformed and financial behavior changed drastically. I have been able to experience many of these changes firsthand, first as an economist and then as a member of senior management, as Salomon Brothers blossomed into the leading trading and underwriting firm in many of the burgeoning sectors of the credit markets. This firsthand involvement has left its imprint on me. I have experienced near disarray in markets and participated in meetings with government and business leaders during crises, and been part of a business organization that changed from an intimate partnership to a dynamic public corporation.

During my nearly forty years in various sectors of financial markets, I've encountered many brilliant people whom I've admired and of whom I have become very fond. Two of these have had the most influence on my professional career and, to some extent, on my views. They were Marcus Nadler and Sidney Homer.

Marcus was my major professor at NYU, the most memorable teacher I had in my academic career and surely my favorite. I think I can also say that by the time I'd finished my dissertation and received my degree, he was a good friend.

Marcus had a tremendous following in the financial community back in the fifties and early sixties. (He died in 1965 at the age of seventy.) He was one of the first professors to straddle the real and academic worlds, and he did it quite successfully. His course on Current Money Market Problems had an enrollment of several hundred every term, and people took it over and over; I know some who took it more than a dozen times. They'd enroll as special students just to sit in.

There was also the Money Marketeers, a half-professional, half-social organization sponsored by New York University. It was a sort of Marcus Nadler fan club, its membership limited to people who had taken his course. Dinner meetings were held three times a year, and they always ended with a talk by Marcus.

Marcus reminded me of a biblical prophet. He had a resonant voice, a cadenced way of speaking, and when he said something, it was more than a statement: it was a pronouncement. He had an extremely logical mind and a wonderful talent for teaching, for breaking complex concepts down into their component parts and making them understandable. He could simplify and explain the most abstract ideas and then draw out their practical implications. But he was surprisingly modest, despite all the attention he received. "In the land of the blind," he would always say, "the one-eyed man is king."

Another aspect of Marcus that impressed me was his own conviction about the seriousness of his subject. Although he was not closely identified with any particular school of economics, he strongly conveyed the impression that this business of banking and finance and money is a serious matter, not to be taken lightly. He stressed that it plays a significant and crucial role in many aspects of life and ultimately has far-reaching consequences. I also probably identified with his European background. Something in his manner said to his audience that there were days in the past, in Europe, when credit and money were misunderstood, mismanaged, and abused, and this created enormous problems.

Marcus was also unusual as a teacher in that he took a sincere interest in his students. He was always available for advice on career problems, and many of us consulted him on personal matters as well. He was instrumental, for example, in my going to Salomon Brothers. Through Marcus, I met Charles Simon, a senior partner at Salomon Brothers, who introduced me to Sidney Homer. Charles Simon, who became a dear friend, strengthened my views on the need for financial responsibility and integrity and encouraged me to speak out.

Indeed, throughout my career at Salomon Brothers I have always had the opportunity to express my own views regardless of the vested business interests of the firm. I am indebted to my associates for this opportunity and for their confidence in me to

11

say it as I have seen it. They have a rare attitude on this matter. This privilege is accorded to few in business or in public life, where opinions are often filtered to conform to party lines or business goals.

Sidney Homer was another remarkable person. In early 1961 he moved to Salomon Brothers from Scudder, Stevens, and Clark, where he had worked for many years. Late in 1961 he invited me to leave the Federal Reserve Bank of New York and join him in establishing a research department at Salomon Brothers. He was my boss, at least technically, from then until he retired from the firm in 1972, at age seventy. He passed away eleven years later.

Although Sidney had only an undergraduate degree from Harvard, he was a scholar of the first rank. He was an innovator in flow-of-funds analysis and in investigating the behavior of bond price relationships, and of course in analyzing interest rates. His *A History of Interest Rates,* which was first published by Rutgers University Press in 1963 and then in a revised edition in 1975, is still considered a standard work in the field. This book will always be important to me, not just because of the subject matter but also because of my rather intimate involvement with it. Just a few weeks after I joined Salomon Brothers, Sidney came to see me with the galleys of his book in hand. He asked if I would read them for him, which of course I readily agreed to do. But being exceedingly meticulous, he then added that he wanted me to read the galleys *out loud* to my secretary, who would also have a set. I am sure that I am the only person who has ever read aloud (or probably ever will read aloud) 594 pages of text and 81 statistical tables containing interest-rate data from 2000 B.C. to the present.

Charles Simon and Bill Salomon were the two partners mainly responsible for hiring Sidney. Though they were completely unlike him, they understood what he could bring to the firm, how he could add style and character. Sidney represented an unmined area of knowledge, and they realized that if he could bring his knowledge to bear on market developments, Salomon Brothers could gain intellectually and, ultimately, financially.

Sidney had many admirable qualities. I benefited enormously from his detailed knowledge of financial markets and his historical perspective. His style of writing and his behavior were remarkable. He wrote with flair in a grand manner. He never criticized; he suggested. Like Marcus, he plowed through complicated statistical and economic material to unearth meanings and then explained those meanings in understandable language. His advice on my writings was invaluable.

Both Marcus Nadler and Sidney Homer recognized the essential role financial markets play in the prosperity of our society. Surely neither would have approved of some of the changes in financial behavior and the resulting turbulence described in the following pages.

PART II

Financial Markets

CHAPTER 2

Financial Markets Yesterday and Today

To think, just a few decades ago business and financial decisions were made on the assumption of substantial availability of credit, at moderate fixed cost and for maturities from 25 to 40 years. Many recall those days with nostalgia.

Several decades ago, people in the real world—those engaged in production and sales—ruled the roost, while finance took a low priority in business decision making and little attention was paid to investment decisions. Nevertheless, business results then were exceptionally good and investment performance more than satisfactory. Today finance has been given a high priority in business. Investment management is extremely active, and performance is measured frequently. However, the results have not always been commensurate with the effort.

There are many ways of illustrating what has happened in financial markets in the past quarter century. In one sense, the changes that have taken place are encapsulated in the behavior of interest rates. Since interest rates are prices that result from borrowing and lending transactions, they provide a unique measure of financial activity. We will examine interest rates per se in some detail later, but for now I'd like to briefly trace their course for the light they cast on recent developments in financial markets.

INTEREST-RATE DIFFERENCES

The most striking feature of interest rates during the postwar period is how much higher rates are today in comparison to what they were in the fifties and sixties. Two other features of interest rates are also noteworthy: the increase in volatility in recent years and the startlingly high real rates of interest in the early eighties.

Real interest rates are more meaningful than market or nominal interest rates because they take account of changes in the purchasing power of money due to inflation. Of course when there is little or no inflation, market interest rates tell the whole story. Someone lending funds for a year at 10 percent receives back 10 percent more purchasing power than was lent out. But if prices rise by 6 percent during the year, then the lender is repaid in depreciated dollars and cannot buy 10 percent more goods and services when the funds are repaid.

The real interest rate adjusts for inflation by subtracting the annual rate of price increase from the market rate of interest. In this illustration, the market or nominal interest rate is 10 percent, but the real rate is only 4 percent—the 10 percent market rate minus the 6 percent rate of inflation. In an inflationary era, real rates are clearly more significant than unadjusted market rates.

In theory, real rates should be measured as market interest rates minus *expected* inflation, because expectations about future inflation definitely affect market interest rates. If an acceleration of inflation is generally expected, lenders will probably be less eager to lend, and borrowers more eager to borrow, thereby driving market rates higher. On the other hand, if everybody expects inflation to diminish, then lenders will probably want to lend more, but borrowers will want to borrow less. So market rates fall.

However, expectations are difficult to measure, and in practice real interest rates are conventionally measured not as market rates minus expected inflation but rather as market rates minus the rate of inflation that has actually occurred.

In 1983–84, for example, the real rate of return on long-term high-grade corporate bonds averaged 8.2 percent, consisting of an 11.9 percent nominal market rate of interest minus a 3.7 percent rate of inflation as measured by the GNP (Gross National Product) deflator. This compares with an average real interest rate of about 1 percent for all the previous post–World War II years.

In fact, real interest rates have varied more than is generally realized over the time span of the entire twentieth century. From 1900 through 1984, annual real rates of return—the yield on high-grade corporate bonds less the GNP deflator—averaged 1½ percent, with an average of 2 percent preceding World War II and 1⅓ percent thereafter. Until the last few years, real interest rates fluctuated more widely *before* World War II than after.

There is no evidence of constant real rates of return; real rates vary considerably (see Chart 1) despite the widespread belief that a 2 to 3 percent real rate of return is in some mystical way the norm. Even ten-year averages have ranged from a minus 3.8 percent to a plus 5.8 percent.

Many attribute the high real interest rates of the eighties to inflationary expectations. As discussed above, changes in expectations about inflation are likely to alter borrower and lender be-

19

Chart 1. Real Interest Rates, 1950–85

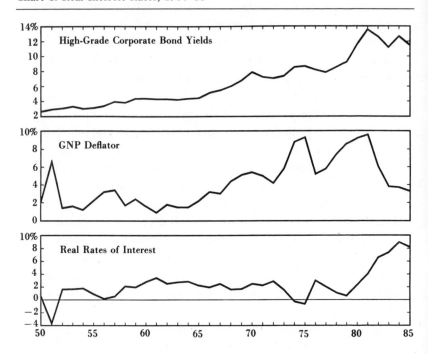

havior. Personally, I have never been completely satisfied with this explanation; it relies too much on projecting the most recent economic behavior or utilizing surveys of questionable reliability. In any event, I believe that the primary explanation for today's high interest rates lies elsewhere—in the new structure of our credit markets and in our monetary and fiscal approaches.

THE INSTITUTIONAL CREDIT STRUCTURE

In the last twenty years, our credit markets have been revolutionized by financial deregulation that sparked an enormous innovative drive and by an unprecedented entrepreneurial zeal among financial participants. The result has been a very large growth of debt in the United States, to $7.1 trillion at the end of 1984 as compared with only $1.5 trillion in 1970.

This debt creation was facilitated by the shifting of typically local and regional credit demanders, such as home buyers, into the national securities markets through the use of many new types of highly marketable securities. A modern-day Rip Van Winkle returning to the credit markets would be astounded at the variety of credit instruments at his disposal. To mention a few: negotiable CDs, floating-rate obligations, Euro-obligations, zero coupon bonds, GNMAs, mortgage appreciation securities, variable-rate mortgages, financial futures, bond options, money market funds, NOW accounts, foreign currency bonds, indexed bonds, and bonds bearing warrants to buy additional bonds! (Tables 1 and 2 provide further detail on recent financial innovations.)

This rapid debt creation was stimulated further by the introduction of variable-interest-rate financing. Variable rates free the institutional lender from interest-rate risk in lending and encourage him to speed ahead with spread banking, a now well-known process of borrowing funds and investing them at a fixed rate spread over cost. Consequently, rising interest rates no longer impede the innovative institutional lender from increasing asset size and potential profit opportunities.

Interest-rate risk used to be an inhibiting and constraining element in the financing process. Rising interest rates would increase the costs of financial intermediaries, since they would have to pay more to acquire funds. But their fixed-rate assets would still be yielding the old interest rate that was agreed upon back when they were acquired. With variable asset rates, however, the institutional lender blithely receives higher rates on his assets in step with higher costs on his liabilities, so that previous fixed-rate constraints no longer exist.

Table 1. Financial Innovations, 1970–82

Types	(a)	(b)	(c)	2	3	4	5	6
A. Cash Management								
1. Money Market Mutual Funds	✓							
2. Cash Management/Sweep Accounts	✓				✓			
3. Money Market Certificates	✓					✓		
4. Debit Card	✓				✓			
5. NOW Accounts	✓							
6. ATS Accounts	✓				✓			
7. Point of Sale Terminals					✓			
8. Automated Clearinghouses					✓			
9. CHIPS (Same Day Settlement)					✓			
10. Automated Teller Machines					✓			
B. Investment Contracts								
(i) Primary Market								
1. Floating Rate Notes				✓				
2. Deep Discount (Zero Coupon) Bonds	✓		✓	✓				
3. Stripped Bonds	✓		✓	✓				
4. Bonds with Put Options or Warrants	✓			✓				
5. Floating Prime-rate Loans				✓				
6. Variable-rate Mortgages				✓				
7. Commodity Linked (Silver) Bonds				✓				
8. Eurocurrency Bonds	✓						✓	
9. Interest-rate Futures				✓				
10. Foreign Currency Futures							✓	
11. Cash Settlement (Stock Index) Futures						✓		
12. Options on Futures				✓		✓		
13. Pass-through Securities						✓		
(ii) Consumer-Type								
1. Universal Life Insurance				✓				
2. Variable Life Policies		✓						
3. IRA/Keogh Accounts			✓			✓		
4. Municipal Bonds Funds			✓			✓		
5. All-Saver Certificates	✓					✓		
6. Equity Access Account		✓		✓				

Exogenous Causes[a] (columns grouped: 1 = (a), (b), (c))

Table 1. Financial Innovations, 1970–82 *(Continued)*

| | Exogenous Causes[a] | | | | | | | |
| | 1 | | | | | | | |
Types	(a)	(b)	(c)	2	3	4	5	6
C. Market Structures								
1. Exchange-traded Options								✓
2. Direct Public Sale of Securities								
Green Mountain Power Co.			✓					
Shelf Registration			✓			✓		
3. Electronic Trading								
NASDAQ					✓			
GARBAN				✓				
4. Discount Brokerage						✓		
5. Interstate Depository Institutions					✓	✓		
D. Institutional Organization								
1. Investment Bankers/	✓			✓				
Commodity Dealers Salomon/								
Phibro, Goldman Sachs/								
J. Aron, DLJ/ACLI								
2. Brokers/General Finance								✓
Shearson/Amex, Bache/Prudential,								
Schwab/Bank of America								
3. Thrifts with Commercial Banks	✓			✓		✓		
4. Financial Centers (Sears Roebuck)								✓

Source: William L. Silber, "The Process of Financial Innovation." *The American Economic Review,* May 1983, p. 91.
[a]Column headings: 1 = Inflation; (a) = Level of Interest Rates; (b) = General Price Level; (c) = Tax Effects; 2 = Volatility of Interest Rates; 3 = Technology; 4 = Legislative Initiative; 5 = Internationalization; 6 = Other.

VOLATILITY AND MONETARISM

Besides the credit markets' growth in size and diversity, a major force behind high *and volatile* rates was the adoption of a quasi-monetarist approach by the Federal Reserve from October 1979 to late 1982 and to a lesser extent since. Monetar-

Table 2. Financial Innovations in 1985[a]

Instruments	Description
International Markets	
Floating-Rate Coupon Securities	
• Capped	Upper limit on coupon reset rate.
• Mini/Max	Upper and lower bounds set.
• Mismatched	Coupon reset and coupon payment occur at different frequencies.
• Partly Paid	After initial payment for first part of an issue, purchaser must subscribe to future tranches.
Nondollar FRNs	Introduction of deutsche mark- and yen-denominated FRNs.
Nondollar Zero-Coupon Bonds	Introduction of deutsche mark-, Swiss Franc-, and Japanese yen-denominated issues.
Shoguns	U.S. dollar bonds issued in Japan.
Sushis	Eurobonds issued by Japanese entities that do not count against limits on holdings of foreign securities.
Yen-Denominated Yankees	Yen bonds issued in U.S. market.
ECU-Denominated Securities	Increased utilization in U.S. markets; introduction of issues in Dutch and Japanese markets.
Dual-Currency Yen Bonds	Interest paid in yen, principal paid in other currency at a specified exchange rate.
"Down-Under" Bonds	Increased utilization of Euro-Australian dollar and Euro-New Zealand dollar bond issues.
Domestic Markets	
Variable-Duration Notes	At coupon payment date, holder elects either to receive coupon or an additional note with identical terms.
Zero-Coupon Convertible	Zero-coupon bond with option to convert to common stock.

24

Table 2. Financial Innovations in 1985[a] *(Continued)*

Instruments	Description
Collateralized Securities	
• Multifamily Pass-Through	Pass-throughs collateralized by multifamily mortgages.
• Lease Backed	Collateralized by leases on plant and equipment.
• Automobile Backed	Collateralized by automobile loans.
• Revenue Indexed	Mortgage-backed security in which interest payments are augmented by a percentage of issuer's gross earnings.
Commercial Real Estate	
• Finite-Life Real Estate Investment Trust	Portfolio of real estate equities with a specific date by which the portfolio must be liquidated.
• Commercial Mortgage Pass-Throughs	Pass-throughs collateralized by commercial mortgages.
• Cross-Collateralized Pooled Financing	Pooled securities allowing recourse to other mortgages in the pool.
• Rated, Pooled Nonrecourse Commercial Mortgage	Publicly rated nonrecourse real estate-backed bonds.
Tax-Exempt Securities	
• Daily Adjustable Tax-Exempt Securities	Puttable long-maturity bonds with coupon rate adjusted daily.
• Zero Coupon	Zero-coupon tax-exempts.
• Capital Appreciation Bonds	Zero-coupon bonds sold at par or better.
• Stepped Tax-Exempt Appreciation on Income-Realization Securities	Zero-coupon bonds for an initial period, after which they are converted to interest-bearing securities.
• Municipal Option Put Securities	Puttable bonds with detachable puts.
• Periodically Adjustable Rate Trust Securities	Participant certificates based on tax-exempt commercial mortgage loans.
Futures and Options	
Municipal Bond Contract	Introduction of futures contract to tax-exempt market.

Table 2. Financial Innovations in 1985[a] *(Continued)*

Instruments	Description
Options on Eurodollar Futures	Introduction of exchange-traded options on futures to the short end of yield curve.
Options on Treasury Note Futures	Introduction of exchange-traded options on futures to intermediate section of yield curve.
Japanese Government Yen Bond Futures	Introduction of Japanese financial futures contracts.
ECU Warrants	Introduction in Europe of publicly offered and listed options on ECU.
European-Style Options	Introduction in U.S. of options that can only be exercised at expiration. In addition, currency strike prices are in European rather than American terms.
Range Forward Contract	A forward exchange contract that specifies a range of exchange rates for which currencies are exchanged on the expiration date.
U.S. Dollar Index	Introduction of a futures contract on the dollar's trade-weighted value.
Options on Cash Five-Year Treasury Notes	Introduction of options to this sector of the yield curve.

[a]Instruments that were either introduced or became widely used during 1985.

ism produces rate volatility because rates must be taken to whatever level is required to hit a targeted growth for the money supply.

Monetary policy-making had been dominated by an eclectic quasi-Keynesian approach to the economy ever since Marriner Eccles had been appointed chairman of the Board of Governors by President Franklin D. Roosevelt in the thirties. For more than four decades, the Federal Reserve had tried to influence interest rates, the money supply, the quantity of credit, and the foreign exchange rate, sometimes emphasizing one of these variables and sometimes another. While the monetary authorities had considered their mission of the utmost importance, they never labored under the misapprehension that the money supply was the *only* factor that determined GNP, employment, and the pace of inflation. Among the other factors that the Fed always considered important in influencing the course of the economy were fiscal policy, debt management, interest rates, the volume and composition of credit, and union and corporate wage-price policies.

Monetarism, on the other hand, represents a more doctrinaire approach to monetary policy-making. Monetarism stems from the Quantity Theory of Money, which has a long tradition in the history of economic thought. It views the money supply as the main —if not the sole—factor determining GNP, employment, and the rate of inflation. Monetarists thus believe that the Federal Reserve has a relatively simple job: the Fed should target the money supply, permitting it to grow strictly in line with potential real economic growth, and let everything else—including interest rates and the volume of credit—take care of themselves.

In other words, according to monetarism, the Fed should not take interest rates, credit growth, wage-price developments, or international factors into account in determining its policies: the money supply, and only the money supply, is all the Fed should consider. (The fact that there are several different money supplies, often moving in different directions, is generally dismissed by monetarists as unimportant.)

The closer the central bank adheres to the tenets of monetarism, the more volatile interest rates tend to be. The growth of money does not respond to small changes in interest rates. Therefore, monetarism initially has a massive effect on short rates. But long rates cannot remain immune. Volatility thus

27

permeates the entire yield curve, and an unusual meeting of minds occurs between lender and borrower: both prefer to stay short. This, of course, further weakens the credit structure because of the absence of long-term commitments.

In support of the Federal Reserve's policies, however, it must be said that the Fed has had to bear the entire burden of extricating the United States from a dangerous inflationary spiral. A heavy dependence on monetary policy for that purpose will extract its toll in the form of high interest rates. A helping hand from fiscal policy in the form of a smaller deficit, or no deficit at all, would have made for a much softer landing.

THE BUDGET DEFICIT

Which brings us, of course, to another important reason for the high level of interest rates: our expansionist fiscal policy. The controversy over the U.S. Government's huge budget deficit has become rather bizarre. Some conservatives argue that budget deficits don't matter. Several officials of the Reagan administration have denied any linkage between interest rates and budget deficits. Others claim the only thing that matters is the money supply.

Unfortunately, the new emphasis placed on economic quantification obscures the most profound aspect of the federal budget: the budget is the document that represents the social, economic, and financial priorities of the nation. In a democracy, the budget reflects how well these priorities are set and managed. Like no other official document, the federal budget reveals our economic morality, our willingness to accept discipline, and our capacity to respond quickly to changing financial and economic conditions. The budget, set through the democratic process, says more about this nation, and what conditions it will tolerate, than any other measure.

While timely fiscal responses often have been lacking in U.S. national policies, fiscal policy took on an added risk several years ago. At that time, in 1981, we opted for large tax reductions and substantial increases in military outlays without a concomitant slowing in other types of federal government spending. The result has been record-breaking budget deficits; even an extended sharp improvement in economic activity would still leave a large structural deficit.

The large tax reduction passed in 1981, and its consequences, offer sorry testimony regarding the influence of fashion in economic analysis and policy-making. The tax legislation was enacted on the basis of "supply side" economics, a point of view that at the time was nowhere in evidence in the economics textbooks used in graduate or undergraduate schools throughout the United States. Rumor has it that a university professor sketched a diagram on a dinner napkin showing that lower tax rates would generate so much economic growth that the result would be an *increase* in tax receipts. On that basis, with no additional theoretical or empirical evidence, Congress bought the 1981 tax package—and has been regretting it ever since.

In the halcyon years between 1950 and 1966, the federal budget deficit averaged less than 1 percent of GNP. The average was 1.2 percent of GNP in 1967–74 and 2.4 percent in 1975–81. For 1982–86, however, the deficit averages 5 percent of GNP. In addition, the structural deficit, measured on the basis of a 6 percent unemployment rate, averages $105 billion per annum for 1982–86, or 2.6 percent of GNP. By comparison, structural deficits averaged no more than 1.5 percent of GNP in the seventies (see Chart 2).

The conventional notion seems to be that reductions in budget deficits will automatically lower interest rates significantly. I do not share this view. The effect of a budget deficit on interest rates depends, fundamentally, on the phase of the business cycle—whether we are in recession, expansion, or boom.

Small deficits during business recessions contribute to sharp declines in interest rates. This is because in the absence of demands for private credit—which typically shrink in recession

29

Chart 2. Unified Budget Deficit and as a Percentage of GNP for Fiscal Years 1960–85 (Dollars in Billions)

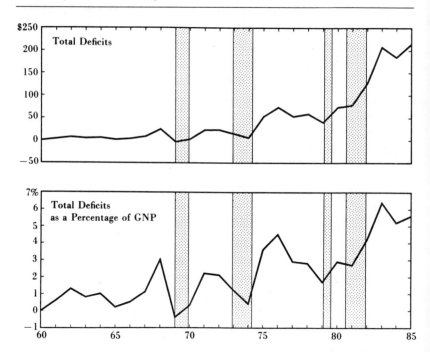

periods—and with only moderate federal government economic stimulus, monetary policy must strive to get the economy going again. It can do this only by providing ample reserves and by lowering interest rates enough to reignite economic activity.

On the other hand, when budget deficits are large during recessions the justification is that monetary policy cannot adequately stimulate the economy. I doubt that monetary policy is impotent; a dynamic economy like ours has an underlying expansionary bias that responds quickly to lower interest rates. When deficits are large, they stimulate the economy through enlarged federal government spending or by tax reductions.

While interest rates fall during recessions, the decline is limited by the increased demand for credit by the federal government.

The Treasury's argument to the effect that deficits in past recessions did not prevent interest-rate declines misses the point. The Treasury should pose the question thus: How much more would interest rates have fallen if the budget deficit had been, say, half of what it was?

The huge budget deficit of the last few years has destroyed the opportunity to enjoy much lower interest rates. While there was a severe recession, with double-digit unemployment rates, we opted for unprecedented fiscal deficits that hampered the responsiveness of monetary policy. Without such deficits, interest rates would have fallen much lower; these record deficits ensured a huge supply of new Government securities that filled the vacuum created by the only moderate supply of bonds issued by the private sector.

The impact of budget deficit reductions on interest rates once the economy reignites is a different matter. Under these conditions, lower budget deficits would probably have a salutary effect on interest rates for only a short period of time.

Imagine the events that would most likely transpire if sizable budget deficit reductions were legislated when the economy is moving upward in expansion. First, both stock and bond prices would probably rise sharply in response to budget cuts, even if there were a brief slowing in the pace of economic activity. Second, the initial dramatic decline in rates would spur new home building and business capital outlays. Thus enlarged private credit demands would eventually replace those of the federal government. Interest rates would then climb again as this borrowing transformation (from government to private borrowing) takes hold, and within six months or so, they might return to the levels that prevailed prior to the deficit reduction.

Because I am known as a strong advocate of lowering the budget deficit, some are startled when I say that budget deficit reductions during business expansions do not cyclically reverse the upward direction of interest rates. However, such reductions do result in other important benefits.

For one, the expansion is likely to be prolonged to the extent that interest rates fall and remain below the levels that prevailed before the deficit reduction. It is difficult to quantify the length of time, because both the size of the deficit and the way it is financed must be considered.

In addition, lower deficits are likely to enhance the quality of a business expansion, especially if deficit reduction is arrived at through cutbacks in expenditures. It will allow new private investments to take the place of those federal government outlays that favor consumption or of those military outlays (if they are reduced) whose economic and social benefits are dubious.

It has been pointed out that some federal government outlays are for investment purposes, that a false distinction is often made between investment and consumption, and that many private investments are more wasteful than a lot of federal government investments. Much is valid in these arguments. Nevertheless, private investment *is* subject to the discipline of the marketplace, while federal government spending is not. Successful private capital outlays generate profits, while unsuccessful outlays are a cost to society and are discarded quickly through losses. What force acts as a discipline to federal government capital outlays if there is no pressure to reduce the budget deficit?

Having discussed the significance of budget deficits for interest rates during recessions and business expansions, I want to turn to their significance during economic boom periods, the final and most challenging phase of the business cycle.

By definition, booms are typically periods of intense competition for limited funds. The sectors that are most vulnerable to interest rates—housing and capital spending—are eventually curtailed by rising rates. The titanic struggle between the demands of business and those of government is resolved in favor of the latter, at the cost of cutting back private investments of long duration.

In the process, rates usually rise well above general expectations. In contrast to the varying responsiveness of the major private sectors to interest-rate changes, federal government credit demands are insensitive. Given large deficits, the cyclical height of economic activity can do nothing but propel interest rates sharply higher.

We must be more realistic and recognize the magnitude of the task facing monetary policy when it is encumbered by enormous federal deficits. Because large U.S. Government financing needs are not sensitive to interest-rate movements, rates have to rise more than they would otherwise in order to limit the capital demands of the private sector as higher levels of business activity are attained. At a minimum, the intransigence of federal government deficits limits the flexibility of monetary policy-makers.

Some claim that abuse of the federal budget can be neutralized to a large extent by a disciplined monetary policy. Even if this were technically feasible, should we, as a nation, expect a dozen members of the Fed's Open Market Committee to be omniscient and remedy the fiscal laxity, manifested by the deficit, that all of us seem willing to condone?

CHAPTER 3

Dangers in the Rapid Growth of Debt

As previously discussed, debt in the United States has been growing by leaps and bounds in helter-skelter fashion. Such attempts as there have been to formulate some more orderly policy pertaining to debt are in a morass.

They are in a morass in part because strong vested interests are at stake. Banks and other financial institutions, basking in the illusion of riskless "spread" banking—where the interest-rate risk is passed on to the borrower—press for more freedom from restrictions that would inhibit their growth. After all, no one wants to be regulated or disciplined. Borrowers also prefer liberal terms to strict terms and credit accommodation over denial. Savers, having tasted the elixir of high interest rates that has accompanied financial deregulation, similarly favor the new, less restricted financial life. They are not interested in the risk-taking engaged in by financial institutions to whom they have entrusted their savings, as long as the U.S. Government guarantees the safety of those funds.

The false comfort provided by the credit creation process is part of the problem. The generation of credit is of course quite agreeable. Borrowers can act on business decisions or fulfill personal or public needs. Lenders expect to profit from the transaction. The initial credit creation process contributes to economic expansion and financial exhilaration.

Once the debt is created, however, it may become sufficiently onerous to the borrower to necessitate changes in the repayment schedule. There may be failures or partial refinancings. When credit difficulties arise in the repayment process, near-term or emergency measures are put into effect rather than more fundamental long-term solutions.

This chapter describes some disturbing dynamics of the expansion of debt, the weaknesses or danger signals that are manifesting themselves in the credit structure, the forces responsible for our ballooning debt, the issues confronting national policy-makers today, and some suggested policy responses.

RAPID DEBT GROWTH

U.S. credit market debt—primarily of households, governments, and businesses—totaled an estimated $7.1 trillion at the end of 1984, up from $2.4 trillion ten years ago and less than $1 trillion in 1964. Debt grew by 7.3 percent annually during the ten years ending in 1969 and by 11.1 percent in the subsequent decade. It slowed briefly in 1982 but then gained new momentum in 1984, increasing at a record 14 percent rate.

One disturbing aspect is that debt is increasing more rapidly than nominal gross national product is. Compared with the $7.1

trillion in credit market debt, nominal GNP was $3.7 trillion in 1984 (see Chart 3). Credit market debt thus exceeded GNP by a ratio of almost 2:1. This ratio was 1.7:1 in 1974 and 1.6:1 in 1964. Clearly, a pronounced widening of this gap has occurred in the past five years.

Even so, these estimates understate matters, because there is a sharply expanding hidden debt for which no aggregate data are available. This includes, for example, futures, options, interest-rate swaps, currency swaps, credit guarantees by banks and insurance companies, and lines of credit. In addition, debt growth may be disguised by accounting conventions that permit

Chart 3. Nominal Gross National Product and Credit Market Debt Outstanding, 1960–85 (Dollars in Billions)

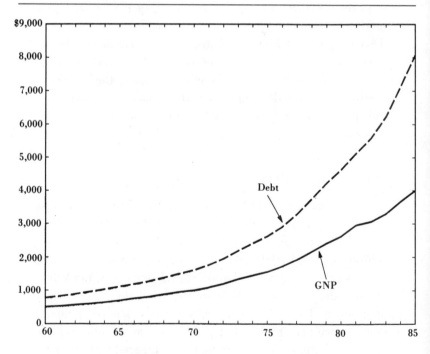

the netting out of many assets and liabilities. If we could calculate the total of *gross* liabilities, then the credit structure would be much larger than has been estimated. In other words, borrowers, financial intermediaries, and others probably employ greater leverage of debt to capital than is discernible, given current balance-sheet conventions.

Since the beginning of the sixties the level of liabilities for all major categories of borrowers has of course risen. It is worth special mention, however, that in the past ten years the U.S. Government has posted the biggest percentage increases in borrowing. Outstanding government debt grew by about 3 percent annually in the sixties, by about 6 percent annually from 1970 through 1974, by 11 percent from 1974 through 1979, and by about 13½ percent annually from 1979 through 1984.

DANGER SIGNALS

Looking inside this bloated debt structure reveals a number of dangerous forces that will aggravate economic and financial instability:

1. There has been a marked increase in *short-term* borrowing by the private sector, particularly by business firms. Short-term borrowing means that the debtor firms have to be continuously prepared to repay their indebtedness, running the risk of illiquidity problems virtually all of the time. It also means that rising interest rates hurt such firms first.

2. Closely related to this development is the private sector's increasing willingness to finance at floating interest rates and to shorten the maturity of borrowings from long-term to medium. Both actions to finance at the cheapest end of the yield curve assume that the inherent risk of sharply rising interest rates will not occur or will not endure for long or can be passed along.

37

3. State and municipal governments are also liberalizing their financing strategies by shifting down in the maturity of their financing. They are issuing a greater volume of short-term paper as well as puttables, which in many cases can be sold back to the issuer on a demand or seven-day basis. Not too long ago, puttables were considered an unacceptable way of financing.

4. With increasing reliance on short- and medium-term borrowing, the traditional long-term bond market (with maturities of twenty-five years or longer at fixed rates) is diminishing in importance. Hard as it may be to believe, it was once the hallmark of the American bond market.

5. What is left of the traditional long-term bond market has mainly become the domain of the U.S. Treasury. Because of its huge issuance of long bonds, the federal government has saturated this market, and as a result private borrowers have moved to shorter maturities. Thus the private borrower, who can least withstand upward leaps in interest rates, has become a greater risk taker, while the U.S. Treasury, the most creditworthy, has usurped the long-term fixed-rate market.

6. Another ominous development has been the recent failure of the equity market to provide a significant net new source of capital for business. Following a record volume of equity issuance in 1983, the equity base of U.S. corporations actually contracted in 1984 as a result of stock retirements (reflecting mergers, acquisitions, and leveraged buyouts). These retirements totaled over $100 billion; as a result, the addition to corporate debt exceeded the addition to equity (retained earnings plus net new equity issuance) by a record margin, reestablishing an unwholesome trend that first became noticeable in the seventies (see Chart 4).

Arguably, this contraction or retirement of shares makes available equity more scarce and therefore supports equity

Chart 4. Net Changes in Nonfinancial Corporate Debt and Equity, 1960–85 (Dollars in Billions)

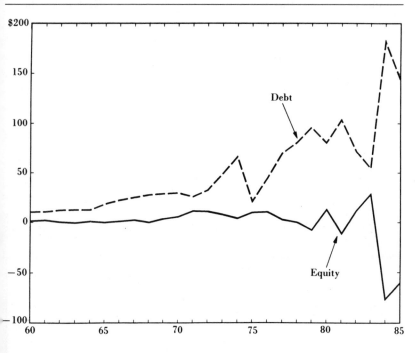

prices. In a narrow sense this is true, but in the long run it would be accurate only if the growth of debt were to slow down. Continuous rapid debt expansion inhibits share values because of the mounting debt burden it inflicts on corporations and because investors are offered a wide-ranging menu of fixed-income investments as alternatives to equities.

As an illustration, think of the $7 trillion credit market debt and the massive ongoing growth of debt that must be cleared through the market on competitive terms. Furthermore, consider how it is effectively merchandised through the use of new credit vehicles, attracting the funds of households directly and of financial intermediaries.

Massive debt creation tends to limit equity market performance. The historical relationship between the stock market's performance on the one hand and credit/debt expansion on the other clearly supports this position; as Chart 5 indicates, the market value of shares rose in near lockstep with the *moderate* growth of debt in the early and mid-sixties, but since then has been in the shadow of the debt market most of the time.

7. Price or interest-rate volatility is still another feature that has accompanied the massive growth of debt. The annualized daily price change of long Governments was 11 percent in 1984

Chart 5. Credit Market Debt Outstanding and Market Value of Outstanding Equities, 1960–85 (Dollars in Billions)

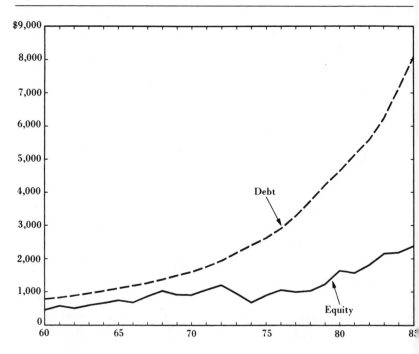

as compared with volatility only a third as large in the mid-seventies.

To be sure, the heightened volatility reflects the Federal Reserve's somewhat more monetarist policy approach, as explained in the previous chapter, but it has also resulted from the bloated debt structure. Volatility is enhanced by huge debt rollovers, increased leverage through futures and options, and the increasing sensitivity of performance-oriented investors to near-term developments. Portfolio managers have to succeed quickly or find other lines of employment as investors shift funds in search of the best short-term performance.

8. While many of the new proxy or hybrid credit instruments are designed to help market participants cope with volatility, they also have negative influences. Some have grown enormously in size. For example, the average daily volume of transactions in U.S. Government note and bond futures totaled $16 billion in the first half of 1985, close to 80 percent of the cash transactions in outstanding Government issues with maturities over five years. This compares with $12.5 billion, or 61 percent, for all of 1984. Trading in currency options has increased nearly eightfold since 1983, the first full year in which they were offered. Average daily open interest in options on Government bond futures was $20 billion, compared with less than $5 billion in 1983, also their first full year of trading.

The negative aspects of these instruments can be described as follows. While their purpose presumably is to reduce risk, not all transactions are perfect hedges and not all arbitrages work as anticipated. This type of activity tends to enlarge asset and liability positions and thus increases the need for improved risk-control management.

In addition, the highly developed futures market in Governments gives this segment a great advantage over the corporate and municipal sectors. Municipal futures, which are still small in size, came into being only recently. The Government futures market facilitates the distribution of new U.S. Treasury issues and increases the depth of the secondary market. If, by chance, credit quality deteriorates in the private sector, this comparative advantage of Governments would become even more pronounced.

9. The last danger signal associated with this rapid swelling of debt is the fragility of many of our financial institutions. Their assets and liabilities have risen much more quickly than their capital accounts. For some institutions, capital would vanish—and even be negative—if assets were liquidated to honor liabilities. While their currently stated capital may meet regulatory accounting standards, it does not meet the test of the marketplace, because their assets are not written down to market value. Institutional liquidity now depends more on the capacity to borrow than on holdings of short-term self-liquidating assets.

FORCES THAT ENCOURAGE CREDIT EXPANSION

None of the above-mentioned developments have come into existence suddenly. They have evolved over many years during which financial institutions and the entire framework of the financial market exploded in size and changed its character.

The forces behind these developments are diverse. It is too easy to attribute the expansion in debt entirely to misdirected monetary and fiscal policies. To be sure, as supervisors of our credit structure, at least in name, governmental monetary and fiscal authorities must bear the largest part of the responsibility. But other forces have also contributed.

For example, debt no longer carries the stigma attached to it by earlier generations who survived the Great Depression. The absence of such a disaster in the postwar period has served to comfort borrowers and lenders and encouraged them first to increase their borrowing and lending and then to maximize its usage to help bolster living standards—to satisfy rather than postpone economic gratification. It is no longer cause for celebration when a home mortgage is finally paid off. Instead, refinancing of the property is quickly sought.

In the business world, modern financing strategies hardly distinguish between credit and money, between liabilities and liquidity, between liquidity and marketability. The intensive use of financial resources is just one of several approaches used to enhance profits. Indeed, in the seventies and eighties, firms with large financial assets ran and continue to run the risk of takeovers by corporate raiders.

Our tax structure, as is well known, also favors the creation of debt. For both businesses and households, interest payments on debt are generally deductible from taxable income. Most tax shelters are created through the haven of debt. In contrast, on the equity side there is double taxation on corporate income: once at the corporate level and again at the dividend level.

Deregulation of financial institutions has also played a role. Circumscribed in years past by lending restrictions and interest-rate ceilings, financial institutions successfully pressed for greater financial freedom following each of the occasional periods of financial stringency in the past quarter century. The enhanced freedom they won introduced a new entrepreneurial spirit that contributed to the introduction of new financing techniques and credit instruments.

Financial innovation and deregulation have contributed to looser credit standards and to the rapid growth of debt in subtle ways. Through floating-rate issues (i.e., spread banking), financial institutions can insulate themselves against interest-rate risk by quickly passing on increases in their sources of funds to their borrowers. In the past, higher rates restricted debt growth, because financial institutions could not as easily pass higher costs on to their customers. This squeezed institutional profits and curbed the institutions' willingness to acquire new liabilities with which to make new loans and investments.

Today it is the final borrowers—households, businesses, and governments—and not the financial institutions who must absorb the cost of higher interest rates. We therefore now have a mechanism that encourages financial institutions to be highly entrepreneurial. Interest-rate movements are not the key influence on the profits of major financial institutions; rather, the primary factor is the volume of loans and investments in their portfolios. Insulated from the impact of interest-rate swings, institutions try to maximize profits by growth of assets and liabilities—and therefore growth of debt.

Financial institutions and market participants are thus left with credit risk (i.e., risk of possible default). Borrowers do not perceive the danger that exists, for example, in floating-rate financing. The inducement to borrow at the short end of the yield curve is great when the curve is positively sloped—that is, when short-term interest rates are below long-term rates. Market participants generally do not anticipate significant increases in interest rates, and when interest rates do climb, they expect the rise to be brief and the yield curve to return to its usual positive slope rather quickly.

Financial institutions tend to assume that risk diversification —a classic portfolio principle of financial institutions—protects them sufficiently from the negative impact of credit deterioration. In addition, credit risk is blurred by increasing recourse to credit guarantees and insurance. In today's world, institutional lenders and investors take false comfort that their enlarged securitized holdings allow them to make quick adjustments to changes in credit conditions.

For the system as a whole, however, this is impossible. Any single bank or investor can sell off assets to others and raise cash in an emergency, but that means others must be willing to acquire the assets. If *everyone* is trying to raise cash at the same time, no one will be successful, because there will be no buyers.

Indeed, it is this principle that has served for a century as the foundation of central banking; as Walter Bagehot, England's leading financial theorist in the 1800s, pointed out more than a century ago, the central bank's fundamental role is to serve as lender of last resort, an ultimate source of liquidity, when funds are not available anywhere else.

It is also virtually impossible for major market participants to avoid being caught up in the large debt creation process, given the structure of our financial system. If participants fail to adapt to the new world of securitized debt, proxy debt instruments, and floating-rate financing, then they lose market share, make only limited profits, and do not attract the most skilled people. The driving force behind profit generation is credit growth.

As an illustration, our financial system today encourages marginal deposit institutions to enlarge rather than to maintain or to reduce their size. To reduce size would require *not* paying market rates for deposits, thus resulting in a loss of deposits and liquidation of some assets. In many instances this would mean taking an actual loss and thus reducing their already thin equity capital. This is not an acceptable alternative. Therefore, the marginal institution moves in the opposite direction: it bids aggressively for deposits. Then it seeks the highest rate of return by purchasing lower-quality obligations to offset the cost of deposits and to build up its weak capital account.

Our national policy approach is caught in a quandary. On the one hand, the drive in support of financial deregulation still has substantial momentum. On the other hand, a new and not-yet-coherent effort to reregulate has surfaced. At the heart of the debate about deregulation versus reregulation are fundamental issues regarding the role of financial institutions in our economy.

On the one side is the view that financial institutions should be subject to the discipline of the marketplace, to its risks and rewards, and thus prosper or perish as market forces dictate. Others, like me, believe that financial institutions play a unique role as intermediaries between suppliers and demanders of credit. They are holders of savings and temporary funds. Through intermediation, they finance many economically crucial activities. In this function, they must always balance their entrepreneurial drive with their broader fiduciary responsibilities. In other words, they have both a private *and* a public obligation.

In a fully deregulated financial system, this balancing of responsibilities would be fulfilled by the marketplace. Losses, failures, and bankruptcies are the ultimate rebalancing forces in the market. As deregulation has taken hold, however, these market disciplines have, in many cases, *not* been permitted to exert themselves.

When problems have arisen, contractual debt arrangements have been abrogated and lenient terms have been substituted, often with official encouragement. Large debtors and financial institutions have not been allowed to fail. Brazil, for example, received financial aid from the U.S. Government. Continental Illinois Corporation had its liabilities and those of its bank guaranteed, because officials rightfully feared that such a failure would have dangerous financial consequences. Thus we seek the efficiencies of deregulation but refuse to submit to the "prosper or perish" rules of the marketplace.

This is an inconsistency, to say the least, and if prolonged will further accelerate the credit creation process. The risks become blurred when major marginal borrowers and institutions are protected by the federal government; many others are assured funds through credit insurance, letters of credit, or financing arrangements in which surveillance of the debtor is limited.

In this framework, the role of the federal government in periods of financial stringencies is bound to increase. Think of the pressure that households will bring to bear on the federal government someday, when rates on adjustable-rate mortgages and floating-rate consumer loans are driven to lofty levels and the debt burden of the household-consumer sector preempts a large slice of personal income.

POLICY PROPOSALS

Must we return to the rules and regulations that prevailed a few decades ago in order to rein in the growth of debt? Financial markets have changed too much for that. Vast improvements in communications and financial technology have created close linkages within the U.S. credit markets and with markets abroad. Distinctions among institutions have been so blurred that it would be impossible to put Humpty-Dumpty back together again.

We need to implement the best aspects of deregulation and the best applicable safeguards of reregulation. By and large, this will require injecting some friction into the debt creation process —not more lubricants:

1. We must do all we can to ensure continued reasonable economic growth in the United States. A recession would enhance the risk of credit quality deterioration and large debt write-offs. A prolonged economic expansion would allow financial institutions to gradually write off old poor risks, while other marginal borrowers would have the opportunity to rehabilitate themselves.

2. The federal budget deficit should be substantially reduced. If it is not, as we move to a higher level of resource utilization, the huge borrowings of the U.S. Treasury will clash with those of the private sector. This will place an enormous burden on monetary policy, which will then be forced to allow interest rates to rise sharply, with resulting financial shock and economic damage.

3. The federal agencies involved in the supervision and regulation of our financial markets and institutions need to be strengthened. The recent emphasis on monetarism and deregu-

47

lation has had the unfortunate effect of relegating these institutions to a secondary status.

4. The Federal Reserve should continue to play an integral part in supervision and regulation. Its role should not be reduced to simply overseeing the growth of the money supply. The distinction between money and credit is increasingly amorphous, and the impact of monetary policy is not confined to commercial banks. As lender of last resort and in its daily association with the currency and credit markets, the Federal Reserve has a uniquely detailed knowledge of market developments and the actions required to defuse financial emergencies. How would events have unfolded without Federal Reserve involvement in the silver crisis associated with the Hunt Brothers and in the financial difficulties experienced by Drysdale, Penn Square, Mexico, Brazil, and Continental Illinois?

5. One way to force improved discipline on debt growth is through greater and more intensive financial market disclosure. Balance sheets and profit-and-loss statements do not sufficiently reveal certain essential information on which risk judgments must be made. For example, there should be more detailed disclosure by financial institutions about the nature and market value of their gross assets and liabilities and about their many off-balance-sheet items and contingent liabilities. Indeed, some of these liabilities should be included in the computation of minimum capital requirements.

6. The equity capital requirements of all financial institutions should come under closer scrutiny. Higher capital requirements serve at least two useful purposes in a financial system that is biased toward debt growth. First, they cut back debt growth, because higher capital creates a direct cost to financial institutions, in contrast to higher interest rates that are passed along to borrowers. Second, higher capital would provide a better

cushion for the creditors of financial institutions, recognizing to be sure that two institutions with similar amounts of capital can have assets differing considerably in credit quality.

7. Given the rapid growth of marketable, or securitized, debt and market volatility, financial institutions should be required to record their assets at the lower of cost or liquidation value. This would induce more conservative lending and investing practices and ensure a capital account with real value.

8. Government supervisory and regulatory agencies should be encouraged to develop a credit-rating system for their respective financial institutions. These ratings should be publicly disclosed. Such official agencies have more intimate knowledge of financial institutions than do the present private credit-rating agencies. Financial weakness would be noticed and remedied more quickly if official credit ratings were required and made known. The way things work now, changes in credit ratings often are made well after the fact.

9. In general, we should adopt, for the time being, the principle of allowing increased competition in the provision of financial services but not in risk-taking. This would allow deposit institutions, for example, to increase their profits and capital without additional liability burdens and without imposing greater strains on capital.

Some have advocated that risk-taking endeavors, such as the underwriting of securities and the making of secondary markets in a wide range of securities, could be confined to subsidiaries of deposit institutions, therefore meeting the capital needs of the marketplace. But the key issue is whether such subsidiaries of large deposit institutions would be allowed to fail. In view of the extraordinary support that the regulatory authorities gave to the holding company and operating bank of Continental Illinois, the answer can hardly be a categorical yes. Thus another form of credit risk-taking would surreptitiously fall under the umbrella of the federal government and exacerbate the debt creation process.

In conclusion, the rapid growth of debt is one of the most pressing problems of the day. It cannot be solved by fine-tuning monetary policy to narrow money-growth targets. Nor can it be redressed solely by reducing the federal budget deficit, although such action would of course be helpful. What is required is a comprehensive program encompassing a clear-cut definition of the role of credit markets in our society and measures that will blend the best of deregulation and reregulation. To accomplish these ends, however, we will have to subordinate many vested interests for the sake of preserving the integrity of credit—an absolute essential for the preservation of a democratic economic society.

CHAPTER 4

The Integrity of Credit

This chapter continues our discussion of the implications of the excessive growth of debt and credit. (Credit, after all, is the other side of debt; a borrower's debt is a lender's credit.) The integrity of credit is being chipped away by a financial revolution that is helping to lower credit standards and muting the responsibilities of both debtors and creditors.

One reason for this is that we are failing to correctly define the role of financial institutions in our society and how this role can best be performed. Instead, we have responded in ad hoc fashion whenever market forces or strong vested interests have exerted pressure. For the most part, the *long-run* consequences of market, regulatory, and legislative changes have been ignored.

Some of the major adverse credit developments of recent years include the following:

1. Debt has been increasing at an unprecedented pace.
2. Short-term borrowing (mainly floating-rate financing) has been rising rapidly, while long-term borrowing by the private sector has been diminishing significantly in importance.
3. The credit quality of business corporations has been deteriorating; this erosion has been exacerbated by mergers and consolidations in which new debt has been substituted for outstanding equity.
4. The equity base of many financial institutions has grown exceedingly thin, and the quality of their assets has declined. In many instances, the market value of institutional assets has fallen below cost, leaving the liquidation value of institutional capital in serious need of repair.

CREDIT WITHOUT A GUARDIAN

We are drifting toward a financial system in which credit has no guardian. We began moving in this direction when deposit insurance was legislated in the thirties. This measure, generally laudable when viewed against the financial disaster of that period, removed the disciplining link between the creditor of the financial institution (that is, the depositor) and the institution itself. It substituted the *regulator* for the creditor, but such efforts as the regulators have made to demarcate and enforce credit standards have obviously been inadequate. In the meantime, deposit institutions, operating under the umbrella of insurance, have been able to attract funds at rates that vary only slightly from each other and at interest costs that certainly do not reflect differences in credit quality among deposit institutions.

Before federal deposit insurance was instituted, in 1934, a bank's creditors—mainly its large corporate depositors—monitored the quality of a bank's assets. After all, the creditors were at risk should the bank suffer losses or go out of business. Banks with high-quality assets could usually acquire deposit funds more cheaply than their more adventurous competitors, because depositors prized safety and stability.

In this connection, it is worth noting that federal deposit insurance has been performing a different role in recent years from the role it was expected to play when it was first put in place. At that time, deposit insurance was mainly thought of as a means of providing protection for small, presumably unsophisticated depositors who needed a secure place in which to hold their life savings. In line with that limited objective, deposits were at first insured only up to $2,500. The equivalent in terms of purchasing power today, at the current price level, would be about $20,000, not the $100,000 limit that is currently in force.

Deposit insurance still protects small depositors, of course, but in recent years it seems to have shifted its focus from individuals to institutions, from protecting depositors to protecting banks. When large institutions are on the verge of failure, they are generally merged into another institution so that all depositors are protected *in full*, far beyond the de jure $100,000 insurance limit. As a result, neither small nor large depositors need concern themselves with the lending policies and practices of the institutions in which they have put their money. It is not the depositors who are at risk, regardless of the size of their deposit.

The fact that both the Federal Deposit Insurance Corporation and the Federal Savings and Loan Insurance Corporation price deposit insurance on the basis of fixed-rate assessments, without regard for the riskiness of a particular bank's portfolio, enhances the attractiveness of risk taking by insured financial institutions. Conservative minimum-risk banks pay larger than

53

warranted insurance premiums in order to bail out their more venturesome brethren. Such temptations may indeed have contributed to the go-go image of banks in recent years, in contrast to their historically conservative image of caution, prudence, soundness, stability, and safety.

Increased "securitization" of credit obligations is another development that has had unfortunate consequences. Today many financial institutions do not want to be bound to borrowers; they prefer the opportunity to disengage through securitization. After they make the initial loan, they get rid of the obligation by disposing of it to GNMA or some other packager who takes it over. Thus what was a "private" loan becomes part of a "public" marketable security.

This loosens the link between creditor and borrower. In a nonmarketable relationship, the creditor is tied to the borrower for the life of the loan; of necessity, under these circumstances, credit scrutiny at the inception of a loan or investment is likely to be quite intensive. The same degree of credit investigation is not likely to take place when the relationship between lender and borrower is so temporary.

In a securitized arrangement, many market participants fail to distinguish between the essence of liquidity and marketability. Liquidity means being able to dispose of a financial asset at par, or close to it, while marketability provides the holder an opportunity to sell at *some* price. The illusion of marketability is that holders believe they will be able to sell their investments *before* a significant deterioration in credit quality is generally perceived. Thus the initial pressure to be highly circumspect in the creation of the obligation is absent.

Many of the new marketable obligations, moreover, have yet to be tested by adverse business conditions. In addition, the fact remains that the financial system as a whole, and therefore many of the participants, cannot divest from their portfolios credit obligations that are not wanted by the market.

A world of relatively unrestrained credit growth is also encouraged by the use of credit lines and guarantees. These assurances lead investors to make commitments based on the strength of the guarantor and not on that of the borrower. Concurrently, the credit surveillance that the credit insurer provides is not clear, although it is probably not as close as it would be in a direct borrower-creditor relationship. In addition, insurance is usually for only a portion of the risk, and the insurers' credit exposures are often only off-balance-sheet items, deemed contingent risks.

Many of these developments foster near-term investment behavior to the detriment of longer-term investments and of the nation's economic goals. Short- or floating-rate obligations abound. Near-term portfolio performance measurement has increased in importance in the marketplace, and debt leveraging is accelerating. Equity investments turn into purely speculative vehicles instead of helping to finance established, and more important, new and growing businesses.

THE PROPER ROLE OF FINANCIAL INSTITUTIONS

Are financial institutions different from other business firms? In many ways they are, as I briefly noted earlier. They are linked through a network of domestic and international relationships so that the activity and performance of one major institution can set off a series of rippling repercussions for others. Financial institutions also generally have a smaller capital base relative to their total liabilities than other business corporations. Above all, financial institutions have an extraordinary public responsibility. What is more dear to us than our savings? What is more important to the nation as a whole than how these savings are employed to promote growth and stability?

But financial institutions also have an entrepreneurial responsibility—namely, to maximize profits in order to attract and enlarge capital. As a matter of fact, the high leverage potential of financial institutions tends to fuel their entrepreneurial spirit, especially in a deregulated environment. For financial intermediation to work, however, the public's perception must always be that institutions are managed by people who merit public trust and who are dedicated to preserving the integrity of credit. How can this goal be best achieved?

Herein lies the challenge in formulating the overall strategic course for our financial system. There are two directions. What is the best way to discipline financial institutions: through market forces, allowing them to prosper or fail through some form of natural selection; or through close official supervision and/or regulation? There is philosophical support for each position.

Those favoring the discipline of market forces do not believe in the uniqueness of financial institutions or in the implied public trust or responsibility. They believe that the exercise of market discipline alone will not disrupt economic and financial life. Over the past few decades, of course, we have moved in their direction.

Despite the fervor of those favoring market solutions, and their success in convincing others, their approach at critical moments has not been acceptable. As is common knowledge, large institutions simply have not been permitted to fail. When Continental Illinois encountered difficulties in 1984, all depositors and creditors of the bank—and indeed even of the holding company—were given total official protection, well in excess of the legal $100,000 FDIC insurance protection per depositor. Failure was not tolerated because the bank has a myriad of relationships with other institutions, both here and abroad, that would have been damaged. Furthermore, public confidence in financial institutions in general would have been severely shaken, with unknown but possibly serious economic ramifications. The ripple effects of a financial institution's failure can be much greater than those that flow from the failure of a manufacturing or other nonfinancial firm.

Nevertheless, free-market advocates continue to call for a "level playing field" among financial institutions, a superficially attractive proposition that appeals to our sense of fairness and the spirit of competition. However, it fails to take a number of overriding issues into account.

If there is to be a level playing field, are deposit-type institutions willing to forsake federal deposit insurance or access to the Federal Reserve's discount window, neither of which are available to nondeposit institutions? Are we as a nation willing to let large institutions fail? If not, small and medium-size institutions will be competing at a substantial handicap, leading eventually to monopolistic positions by the larger entities. If financial institutions are truly to be on level ground, are they all ready to adhere to common conservative accounting standards that will reveal the true value of their assets?

There is also the serious issue of how conflicts of interest can be avoided if all demarcations are removed. At the extreme, there will be financial institutions that would want to be lenders, equity investors, and underwriters all at once. It is very difficult to successfully manage the simultaneous performance of these functions. There are bound to be compromises within an institution that will deal inequitably with the creditor or equity position.

Certainly the structure of universal banking in Continental Europe can hardly serve as a model. There banks dominate; financial and economic concentration is high and the spawning of new enterprises through venture capital and other enterprising financial institutions is severely limited. Open credit market activity is moderate on the Continent; most transactions take place in the negotiated banking market. Thus, unlike the United States, the open and negotiated financial markets do not have sufficient interplay to serve as a check and balance on both borrower and creditor and also on the direct lender and open market financing.

Some proponents of deregulation and the level playing field approach suggest that these conflicts and inefficiencies can be avoided if many financing activities are shifted to the subsidiaries of financial holding companies. But this is self-deception; after all, the ultimate strength of the subsidiary is still very much dependent on the capital of the holding company and both have one primary motive—to enhance the capital of the overall entity. In addition, bank holding companies enjoy the indirect benefits of deposit insurance and access to the Fed's discount window. Thus they do not exist under the same market discipline—such as failure—as other institutions that do not possess these benefits.

Think also of how institutions are likely to treat each other in a completely deregulated world. The risk is that many would be priced out of the market unless they found attractive access to funds outside their normal channels. This is because large institutions, which currently lend to their smaller counterparts, could easily capture the markets of these other intermediaries by raising lending charges without necessarily withholding credit. The net effect would be a serious squeeze on the profit margins of dependent intermediaries.

In essence, the concept of a level playing field in our financial system is a mirage. The financial system would look more like a zoo with the bars let down, and all of the attendant adverse consequences would follow. In financial life, as in personal life, none of us can perform *all* roles best; the responsibility of each is different and so it is with the trust and responsibilities embodied in a credit relationship.

THE ROLE OF GOVERNMENT

With the onslaught of deregulation, financial innovation, and new technology, government officials have urged private market participants to limit their zeal—as one authority recently put it, "to suppress the drive to reach out for that one last deal or that last basis point of potential profit." These pleas are laudable but ineffective. Market participants cannot avoid being caught up in debt creation. If they turn their backs on the world of securitized debt, proxy debt instruments, and floating-rate financing, they will lose market share, fail to maximize profits, and be unable to attract and hold talented people.

The driving force underlying profits is credit growth, and in the process the most conservative among institutions compromise standards and engage in practices that they would not have dared pursue a decade or two ago. The heroes of credit markets without a guardian are the daring—those who are ready and willing to exploit financial leverage, risk the loss of credit standing, and revel in the present casino-like atmosphere of the markets.

The pervasive and unique role of financial institutions requires that their performance and conduct should not be determined by the market alone. Government should not abrogate its responsibilities in this connection. Unfortunately, financial innovation, new market technology, and ad hoc regulatory responses have recently been in charge of shaping our financial structure —not legislation that incorporates a vision of the role of financial institutions in our society.

Because of their wide-ranging and extensive impact and their interlocking transactional relationships both within the United States and abroad, financial institutions must be effectively regulated through legislation and supervision in order to balance their entrepreneurial drive with their public responsibilities.

To that end, Congress should establish a National Board of Overseers of Financial Institutions. The distinctions among groups of financial institutions are rapidly diminishing. Their markets are not as segmented as they used to be. They often compete directly for funds in highly interest-sensitive markets and employ the same new financing and investing techniques involving complex transactions. To continue keeping responsibility for supervision divided along the segmented lines of institutional groups fails to recognize the realities of today's marketplace, realities that will be even more obvious in the years to come.

Such a board could provide an integrated overview of our major financial institutions. It should promulgate uniform accounting standards and improved reporting procedures for balance sheets and income statements, and require fuller disclosure of information that would be helpful to directors and trustees of institutions and to the public. All supervisory responsibilities should eventually come under its control.

The board should consist of members from the Federal Reserve System, from federal supervisory agencies, and a select number of highly knowledgeable individuals from the private sector. Perhaps in time this board could take on greater importance than the Federal Reserve Board, as the distinction between money and credit continues to blur. Within five to ten years, if financial innovation maintains its current feverish pace, the deposit function may well be difficult to distinguish from other financial transactions. The increased versatility of credit card usage, computer access by many individuals to funds transfers, and virtually instant investment allocations will raise new questions about the validity of targeting some narrowly defined concept of money as a way of influencing economic activity. New concepts of credit and credit usage will probably supplant the orthodoxy of monetarism.

There is also a need to organize a somewhat similar but looser board that will deal with multinational financial institutions. Financial markets do not end at national borders. Today the international flow of funds is immense and accelerating as a result of the securitization of debt obligations, investor preferences, and rapid advancements in communications and in the dissemination of information. If the value of credit is to be maintained, and if credit is to enhance rather than destabilize international economic life, then some sort of cooperative oversight arrangement should be established that would help prevent excessive international risk exposure.

CHAPTER 5

A Disregard for Capital

A disregard for capital is apparent today in all walks of life. It can be seen in governmental policies, in contractual relationships between creditor and debtor, between stockholders and management, and in the language and practices of investments, accounting, and finance. This disregard is evident financially in all three major sectors of the economy—in the federal government, in the business sector, and in the household sector.

MANIFESTATIONS OF THE DISREGARD FOR CAPITAL

One example of the disregard for capital is indicated by the relationship between the growth in outstanding credit market debt—which comprises the liabilities of government, business, and households—and the market value of outstanding equities. I have noted this relationship in discussing how outstanding debt has climbed far above the value of equity (see Chart 5, page 40). At the end of 1984, credit market debt totaled $7.1 trillion and equities $2 trillion, a vast $5 trillion gap. By contrast, as late as 1968 debt totaled $1 trillion and equities $630 billion.

This phenomenon of a rapid growth of debt and relative stagnation of equity values, possibly unprecedented, suggests several points pertinent to the major theme. It suggests, for one, that the growth of inflation is facilitated by an accommodative attitude regarding the issuance of debt, an obliging monetary policy, and a tax system that discourages equity growth.

It also suggests that inflation hurts equities, contrary to the prevailing wisdom of the fifties and sixties. During the fifties and sixties, the standard view of experts, virtually unanimous, was that common stocks were a good hedge against inflation. Accordingly, the bylaws of many trust and pension funds were changed to permit the acquisition of equities in order to safeguard purchasing power. Unfortunately, as is well known, equities peaked in the early seventies in real terms and have yet to regain the levels they reached back then. In nominal terms, the stock market has surpassed its early-seventies levels, but not in real terms.

A second example involves the growing role of the federal government as a demander of credit. Here too, a few statistics tell a powerful story. In the fifties and sixties, the net credit demands of the federal government, including the U.S. Treasury and federal credit agencies, accounted for only 6 percent of all demands financed in U.S. credit markets. They climbed to 14 percent in the first half of the seventies, to 23 percent in the second half, and to a remarkable 38 percent in 1983–84.

The growing credit demands of the federal government are

detrimental to capital because these borrowings have largely financed consumption through transfer payments to the private sector and thus absorbed resources that might have built up permanent capital. Outlays for human resources, mainly transfer payments, now account for 50 percent of all federal budget outlays as compared with 43 percent in 1971 and only 22 percent in 1956.

Some of the increase in government debt is a substitution for private debt. In other words, the disregard for capital is disguised by the government in financing or guaranteeing transactions that would not otherwise be acceptable to private lenders or investors. A false economic validity of projects is thereby fostered. Although substitution of government for private credit has thus far been mainly for financing consumption or housing transactions, it could eventually spread to financing private capital needs as well.

The growth of government borrowings is also disturbing on other grounds. During the early part of a business recovery, such new debt limits the benefits that should accrue to the private sector from an easing in monetary policy. Massive government deficits in this period interfere with financial rehabilitation because they curtail the rise in the value of financial assets, which is an important prerequisite for inducing capital financing. Later, in the more mature stages of a business expansion, large government borrowings exacerbate the conflict in credit markets.

A third example involves business finance. For twenty years after the end of World War II, there was a reasonable consistency in how business corporations financed their growth: for every dollar of new debt, they added a dollar of equity, through a combination of retained earnings and the issuance of new shares. This pattern was broken in the mid-sixties. Since then, debt issuance has risen sharply and the growth of equity has lagged far behind. From 1952 through 1964, nonfinancial corporations increased their debt by $120 billion and their equity by $150 billion; from 1966 through 1984, on the other hand, they increased their debt by $4 trillion but their equity by only $600 billion.

SOCIAL CLAIMS

A fundamental change has taken place in our society over the past five decades, and although on the surface it appears to have run its course, in fact its rate of growth is all that has slowed. Huge social claims have come into existence in the form of transfer payments of governments, private and public pension funds, and governmental regulation, with little regard for the ultimate impact these social costs will have on our productivity, on our international competitive position, and on our individual economic behavior.

One of the principal reasons for the persistence of inflation —even in recessions we don't appear to be able to get the annual rate of price increase much below 4 percent or so—is that these transfers of claims on annual production of wealth have grown to exceed our ability to provide them in real terms.

A democracy oriented toward an unaffordable egalitarian sharing of production, rather than toward an environment of equal opportunity, makes it virtually impossible to impose the ongoing discipline required for long-term stability and growth. Government concern is concentrated on immediate difficulties, while long-term impediments to growth are neglected. National economic policy is now conducted on the premise that we can compartmentalize economic time periods—recessions, recoveries, booms—as though they were uncorrelated entities, so that we can apply appropriate policies to each without regard for the consequences in the next phase. We are fashioning an economic and financial structure to conform with the demands of this kind

65

of society. The transformation is occurring silently and irregularly; only occasionally are there warnings about the drift.

The financial counterpart of this drift is evident in the realities and practices pursued in business and finance. In the harshest sense, a large number of insolvencies is no longer acceptable. By definition, therefore, there is now more than a tendency to keep marginal debtors afloat. Unless borrowers have been cast into legal bankruptcy, creditors seem inclined to preserve their borrowing rights.

More subtle is the increasingly widespread practice of borrowing short to finance long-term requirements. In these instances, the lending and investing institutions preserve the fiction of maintaining their liquidity because the obligation is classified as "short-term," while the borrower acquires funds that cannot be repaid as originally scheduled. This practice is most prevalent in international finance. But it is also increasing domestically, where a significant portion of short-term bank loans and outstanding open-market paper finance long- rather than short-term needs, and where we pride ourselves in the application of off-balance-sheet financing devices.

DEFENDERS OF CAPITAL

It is generally believed that business and the investor are *defenders* of capital, but this is not necessarily so. In the past couple of generations the links between management and stockholders have weakened. Emphasis has shifted from the capital resources of the owner-entrepreneur to the talents and skills of the professional manager. Consequently, most compensation has placed heavy emphasis on up-front rewards and pension and retirement benefits rather than on a manager's ability to make a capital investment. Thus few managements have much capital risk at stake in large corporations.

It should not be surprising to find, therefore, that when tax relief is proposed, American management, in the logic of its stewardship, is a strong advocate of accelerated depreciation and the investment tax credit and is *not* in the forefront of favoring reductions in the capital gains tax or eliminating the double taxation of dividends.

In terms of reversing our disregard for capital, however, changing capital gains and dividend taxation policies may be as or more important than accelerated depreciation and investment tax credits. Accelerated depreciation and investment tax credits have a direct impact on business profits, but capital gains and dividend taxation policies could help revitalize the equity participation that is a requisite for renewed economic growth.

Even as the influence of the powerful large individual stockholder-manager has waned, new stockholder groups have frequently lacked the skills for a participatory evaluation of management decisions. In most instances these stockholders—institutional investors—are inclined to sell their shares rather than question management decisions. Institutional and foreign investors now hold about 34 percent of the market value of U.S. stocks. Two decades ago they held 15 percent.

Our conventions and policies militate against institutional stockholders exerting an ongoing partnership in business management. This is particularly true for the largest institutional investors in stocks: public and private pension funds. I do not share the view of Peter Drucker (*The Unseen Revolution*, Harper and Row, 1976) that pension funds will ultimately control—as opposed to own—American business or will have a profound influence on its management. The institutional portfolio practices of our day stress modern portfolio theory and equity risk diversification, not stockholder-management involvements. In essence, corporate managements are frequently independent trustees of a sort for a silent and often absentee stockholder group.

In contrast, the income egalitarianism of our democracy could not be possible without financial lending institutions becoming more entrepreneurial, because they were led or trapped by events that they could not foresee. Here is perhaps the heart of the matter. Lending and investing institutions are holders of huge amounts of savings. They have an awesome fiduciary responsibility that must temper their entrepreneurial drive, because their liabilities are large and their capital is relatively small.

Today who is there to enforce this fiduciary responsibility? The emphasis on monetarism and deregulation among the monetary authorities and in academic circles has apparently relegated banking regulation and supervision to a secondary status. Academicians teach either monetarism or Keynesianism, plus increasing doses of econometrics, while the study of financial institutions languishes. Monetarists believe that a highly competitive system of nondistinct financial institutions will produce the most efficient allocation of credit, and Keynesians appear to be moving in the same direction.

The regulatory authorities, supported by the managers of financial institutions, adhere to accounting standards for those institutions that were perfectly valid decades ago but hardly come to grips with the way inflation has undermined their fundamental soundness. For example, institutions generally are still permitted to value their fixed-income investments at cost even though these obligations may be selling at a substantial discount in the market. In periods of only cyclical fluctuations in inflation and interest rates, this policy is understandable, because fluctuations in the value of such investments is temporary.

However, when inflation and interest rates tend generally upward over long periods of time, this policy creates fictional rather than meaningful capital in financial institutions. There can be little solace in the fact that an initial outlay will be recovered when an obligation is held to maturity, if in the interim the capital of the institution is eroded because the cost of liabilities has exceeded the rate of return on the asset. The consequence is an actual and realizable net worth of many financial institutions well below the stated and published value.

Hardly anyone speaks fervently today about the importance of capital to financial institutions. Perhaps this is due to the nominal rather than realizable value now shown in the capital account and the knowledge that improving the capital of financial institutions in a real sense will take considerable time. Quite possibly this aspect of the disregard for capital had its origin in the thirties, when Congress legislated deposit insurance in response to the inadequacy of bank capital at that time. This action seemed praiseworthy then; however, deposit insurance coverage, as noted earlier, has even further diminished the significance of capital, especially in the eyes of the public.

Today the managements of financial institutions do not speak of the adequacy of their capital, which used to be a frequent topic of reference, but rather of the efficiency with which they manage assets and liabilities and the coverage of their earnings in excess of possible realized losses.

The increased leverage employed by key financial institutions is a dangerous development because it could invite the eventual politicizing of these institutions. When a small capital base controls a large asset-and-liability structure, as is the case today in commercial banks, the ongoing freedom of these institutions can be maintained only if they demonstrate the importance of their private capital. Otherwise, as Continental Illinois demonstrated, in some future period of financial stringency or economic severity, there may be calls for national ownership.

In addition to financial institutions, the roles of debt and equity in corporate finance—and for that matter in society in general—should be clearly defined, understood, and publicly reinforced.

Specifically, corporate debt can never be a full substitute for equity. Debt involves defined corporate obligations of interest payments and repayment schedules. It is a preemptive factor in corporate cash flow and may limit management flexibility. The abuse of the debt-creation process contributes to corporate failures, and for society as a whole it debauches the essence of economic democracy. Equity, in contrast, allows freedom of decision making and often reflects confidence in society and its political and economic institutions. If we diminish the role of equity, we also invite social and political change. It is not difficult to nationalize businesses as well as financial institutions when their equity base is a small fraction of a nation's composite corporate balance sheet.

Much can be done to resurrect the primacy of equity capital. As mentioned above, the capital gains tax and the double taxation of dividends should be eliminated. In addition, the compensation of senior corporate management should reflect the fortunes of the company. It should not be a one-way street: poor performance should result in the forfeiture of some stock awards, options, and of some favorable clauses in job termination settlements, as well as in reductions in cash compensation.

Also, the Financial Accounting Standards Board, the Securities and Exchange Commission, and other regulatory bodies should promulgate more conservative accounting standards and stricter capital requirements. Such decisions should be widely supported by management—not opposed, as is often the case, by those who are trying to protect near-term profit goals.

Security analysts have a role to play as well. They need to focus more on the capacity of corporations to survive intact throughout the course of a complete business cycle, when a substantial corporate debt burden has been assumed. Analysts should also relate the rate of return that is attained to the level of leverage employed. Presumably, a high rate of return with low leverage represents far better evidence of corporate performance than returns where huge borrowings are an important factor in the rate of return on capital.

Some of these suggestions might be viewed unfavorably because of the possibility of their immediate negative impact on the market value of some companies' shares. Let us hope we can overcome such near-term vested interests, because our economic and political future depends on our ability to enlarge the role of equity capital.

CHAPTER 6

Ferment in Financial Institutions

A huge and complicated financial system now straddles the economic landscape, in contrast to the smaller and tidier structure of earlier years. During the past two and a half decades our major financial institutions have grown into amorphous giants. Unfortunately, much of their extraordinary growth is not due solely to managerial talent and skill. Rather, it also reflects the rapid pace of inflation that we have experienced during many of the years since the early seventies.

A generation ago, we could still speak with mutual understanding about the banking industry, the insurance industry, and so on. Now, however, everyone does what everyone else does, so that instead of the banking and insurance and brokerage and thrift industries, we group them all together under the heading of the financial services industry.

While we have financial institutions that are much larger today than they were a generation ago, the concomitant growth in debt that has taken place throughout the economy suggests that they are *weaker* now than they were then. Inflation has swollen the balance sheets of both ultimate borrowers and financial intermediaries. Many excessive and speculative credit demands have been financed that can never be repaid, and by no means all to third-world borrowers. Bank failures have become more common, and many financial institutions have become more fragile as the rapid growth of debt has eroded capital positions for both financial institutions and final demanders of credit.

This feverish expansion of assets and/or liabilities has intensified the always-latent conflict among financial participants as to how to divide the financial pie—a conflict that has brought into focus the impact on institutions of regulation and innovation.

REGULATION AND DEREGULATION

Financial regulation dates back to our country's early history, although many observers associate the beginnings of regulation with the thirties when many of our best-known rules originated. We often overlook the fact that our Constitution granted Congress the power to coin money and regulate its value; the long and multifaceted history of state regulation of financial institutions; the creation of the National Bank Act in 1863 and then the Federal Reserve System in 1913—all of which long preceded the regulatory wave of the thirties.

And of course regulations pertaining to money, credit, and financial institutions did not get their start in nor are unique to this country. Such legislation has a long history worldwide, and for understandable reasons. Money and credit have a pervasive influence, and financial institutions carry a great public trust. It is not regulation that is new in our time but quite the reverse. The drive to *de*regulate is what is curious and novel when viewed in a historical context.

Advocates of deregulation gained a foothold in the sixties and early seventies, when financial disintermediation first became widespread as market interest rates rose above the Federal Reserve's deposit-rate ceilings (known as Regulation Q). Depositors found themselves unable to get more than 4 percent or 5 percent interest on their deposits, due to Regulation Q, although market interest rates on Treasury bills went to 9 percent or 10 percent.

Frustrated, they withdrew their funds from banks and thrift institutions and bought Treasury bills and other money market instruments on their own. This process, the opposite of what usually happens in the financial system, came to be known as financial *dis*intermediation. Funds moved *out* of financial institutions instead of *into* them.

The Treasury "retaliated" by raising the minimum denomination of Treasury bills from $1,000 to $10,000, hoping to thereby stem disintermediation by confining it to the wealthy. It was thought that investors with less than $10,000 would thereby be shut out of direct Treasury bill purchases and forced back into the banks.

However, what happened, of course, was the invention of a brand-new money market instrument/institution, the money market mutual fund, which specialized in gathering together the funds of many small investors so that minimum denomination no longer mattered. Small investors could in effect buy a portion of a Treasury bill by acquiring money market mutual fund shares. As far as the banks were concerned, however, this was just as much financial disintermediation as if their depositors were buying money market instruments directly.

Disintermediation effectively checked the role of depository institutions in fueling inflation but damaged their profitability in the process. As a result, depository institutions and their traditional borrowing customers began to clamor for reform—by which they meant, naturally enough, deregulation (specifically, at that time, the abolition or at least the modification of Regulation Q). They were joined by the then small but already quite vocal band of economists calling themselves monetarists, who propounded the view that the essence of monetary policy should be control of classically defined money but not of credit creation in total.

They were also joined by many laissez-faire-oriented economists and public figures who advocated deregulation throughout the economy on general philosophical grounds. Financial institutions were seen as no different from airlines, communications industries, and long-haul trucking concerns. It was believed, following Adam Smith, that less government regulation would result in improved performance and a more efficient economy.

The main purpose of regulating financial institutions seems to have gotten lost in the clamor. It has always been, and it still is, to induce financial institutions to adhere to and carry out their *fiduciary responsibilities.*

Unfortunately for the system as a whole, the success of these measures leaves a great deal to be desired. Obviously, they have failed to prevent excessive leveraging and balance-sheet deterioration for many financial institutions. This failure may in part be due to faults in the regulations themselves, although some of the blame may also lie with the traditionally rather weak regulatory enforcement process.

We have always had mixed feelings about authority, and this emerges in the way we write and then enforce (or don't enforce) financial regulations. In any event, by now the urge to deregulate has spread far beyond Regulation Q to encompass just about everything that financial institutions do, where they can do it, and how much they can charge for doing it.

If financial institutions were to be completely deregulated, what would be some of the results? In the broadest sense, more savings would be intermediated. Disintermediation on a large scale would occur only in times of crisis, when confidence in institutions becomes strained. Profit margins would initially shrink under the onslaught of widespread competition among institutions. And regional differences among financial institutions would rapidly diminish.

The dismantling of Regulation Q's interest-rate ceilings and the removal of other frictional impediments in financial markets inhibit the Fed's capacity to manage interest rates. In today's institutional framework, where virtually all near-term funds are priced competitively and many arbitraging incentives exist, it is difficult to implement measures that will change interest rates gradually. Markets continuously probe the Fed's intentions, and market participants tend to make decisions based on their expectations of short-term price fluctuations instead of beliefs regarding longer-term underlying values.

FINANCIAL INNOVATION

Innovation, another factor contributing to the present ferment in financial institutions, is often believed to be a by-product of regulation. Regulation surely encourages innovation—which is often designed to circumvent regulation—in order to increase profits. But innovation is also sparked by the profit motive in the rough-and-tumble atmosphere of *de*regulation. Indeed, financial innovation has accelerated in recent years as both borrowers and lenders have been forced to cope with the vicissitudes of an increasingly diverse and less structured financial environment.

Despite the benefits that frequently flow from innovation, it is naive to think that it always contributes to market efficiency and economic welfare. Some new short-term credit instruments have surely induced borrowers to borrow too much, too short, for too long. The emergence of investment proxies, such as financial futures and options generally, and options on indices of securities specifically, may tend to exacerbate market volatility, diverting attention from the more serious business of saving and investment.

Financial innovation differs importantly from technological change, with which it is often confused. Technological change usually has a long lead time in its development; proprietary rights can be protected; and the commitment to exploit new technology generally requires both skill and real resources over a long period of time. By contrast, financial innovation can be put in place quickly, and since there are no proprietary rights, the exploitation effort is very rapid.

Moreover, the skills required to promote financial innovation can be acquired fairly quickly; in many instances, years of experience do not count. As a result, a new entrant into the field can often exploit financial innovation just about as well as, if not better than, a seasoned veteran. This is because financial innovation is often a break with the past and thus past experience has only limited value.

FINANCIAL INSTITUTIONS ARE UNIQUE

We cannot ignore the truth, developed at considerable pain over many generations: namely, that financial institutions are unique. Generally, the capital of financial institutions is small, while their liabilities are huge. They are expected to embody the essence of integrity, their entrepreneurial drive well balanced by a strong sense of fiduciary responsibility. That is why financial regulation has always been a part of economic development, both here and abroad.

The rationale underlying deregulation stems from the false monetarist belief that a distinction should be made between classically defined money, whose growth the central bank should rigorously control, and credit, which is supposed to be determined by the market. It also stems from the false belief that one industry is much the same as another, so that there is no difference between banking and long-haul trucking.

Because of this twin responsibility—entrepreneurial and fiduciary—some *reregulation* of financial institutions seems unavoidable in the future. What shape these new regulations will take is highly conjectural. Too much has happened to allow a return to the financial structure of the fifties and sixties. Communications and financial technology have created close links within our financial markets and with international credit systems. To clearly define the role of specific groups of financial institutions is not as easy as it used to be.

A bank, for example, is an institution that accepts deposits. At present this is at best a technical definition, considering the growth of money substitutes. Is a money market mutual fund—which accepts deposits and even issues checkbooks to depositors—a bank? There is also a movement underway toward the universal bank that would conduct both a commercial banking and investment banking (or merchant banking) business.

Concurrently, global banking institutions, which have a large international involvement, are a prominent part of the financial scene. How should they be regulated, if at all? Official international institutions are poorly designed to perform this role. On the other hand, individual central banks may be asked to provide safety nets for the activities of their global banks which, in many instances, may involve transactions having nothing to do with the bank's country of origin.

It is difficult to believe that regulation combined with monetary policy can be effective in such a diverse and complex financial world. To completely separate regulation from monetary policy, as we have tended to do in the past, would also be ineffective. Both monetary policy and regulation would probably have to focus on influencing aspects common to most institutions. Two of these approaches, for example, might involve regulation concerning the valuation of financial assets and rules regarding appropriate capital requirements.

If financial institutions were required to value their financial assets at market value, they would probably pursue conservative lending and investing policies more consistently. If the monetary authorities imposed capital ratios on financial institutions varying with monetary policy objectives, financial institutions themselves would be more responsive to policy and not be merely policy conduits.

Such measures would help provide a balancing influence between entrepreneurial drive and fiduciary responsibility. Moreover, the central bank would then have tighter control over the total credit creation process, which currently relies heavily on interest-rate movements. Because financial markets are increasingly linked internationally, more formal arrangements than presently exist among major central banks may also have to be instituted in order to stabilize financial conditions.

MANAGING RISK

In the meantime, managing financial institutions will become more demanding. Decentralization of control will prove dangerous because of the diversity of risk-taking propensities within major financial institutions. Indeed, evaluating risk and reward within financial institutions is likely to become increasingly difficult. Both hedging and arbitraging activities involving domestic and international transactions swell balance sheets, making it difficult to establish prudent rules for leveraging.

While young people in financial institutions attempt to maximize their technical skills early in their careers, as financial innovation brings forth new products and trading techniques, managers have their hands full controlling this youthful zeal. The new technicians try to maximize profits perhaps without due regard for the mission of the institution or for the totality of risk involved. Monitoring performance and evaluating risk-taking thus requires improved management surveillance. Otherwise, the control and destiny of a financial institution may be swept away by shortsighted people lacking historical perspective.

Institutional portfolio management has become increasingly

challenging as the menu of investment alternatives has continually expanded, with many new domestic and international offerings ranging from short to long maturities and from real to financial assets of varying liquidity and quality. Forming judgments among such a huge number of alternatives is bewildering. New instruments that, by definition, have no historical performance record, cannot be analyzed in traditional ways. And if one assumes that financial market volatility is here to stay, making relative value judgments based on historical experience is also endangered by the potential of discontinuity with the past.

On the other hand, the return of more moderate price and rate fluctuations would lead to the resumption of relative value trading and investment practices. Underlying this development would have to be greater stability and more predictable behavior in economics and finance. For the time being, however, portfolio managers will no doubt lean toward decision making based on shorter-run phenomena rather than relying on the longer, more fundamental view that dominated portfolio decisions in the fifties and sixties.

In the final analysis, it would be foolish for financial institutions to believe that they can be immune to the consequences of a poorly performing economy and world order. No credit instrument or trading technique can accomplish such a wonder. The behavior of financial institutions, however, can have an important influence on economic performance. That is why financial institutions cannot ignore their fiduciary responsibilities, why their activities are always under public scrutiny, and why the financial system must be organized in such a way that it helps to stabilize and promote economic activity without dominating or damaging it.

CHAPTER 7

International Financial Problems

So far, I have confined myself to domestic financial matters. International financial problems, however, have also become a matter of widespread concern. In the seventies, when the Organization of Petroleum Exporting Countries (OPEC) was a disciplined and highly effective international price-setting cartel, vast amounts of "petrodollars" poured into OPEC treasuries. The funds that were not spent by the OPEC countries on goods and services were "recycled" through private (largely U.S.) commercial banks to many third-world nations, such as Argentina, Brazil, Mexico, and South Korea, whose industrialization was stalled by high energy costs. The OPEC nations bought large-size bank certificates of deposit and the banks used the funds to extend loans to third-world countries.

Not altogether surprisingly, many of the third-world debtor nations have found it virtually impossible to repay these loans on schedule. As a result, the entire international financial system —and especially the U.S. banking system—is still seriously threatened. One of the most difficult problems of the eighties is what to do about this legacy of the seventies.

Table 3. Foreign Indebtedness of Selected Countries, End of 1984 (Dollars in Billions)

Country	Amount	Percentage of GNP
Brazil	$102	49
Mexico	96	55
Argentina	48	61
South Korea	45	56
Indonesia	31	39
Philippines	27	82
Poland	26	30

Table 4. Selected Banks: Loans Outstanding to Four Latin American Countries, End of 1984 (Dollars in Millions)

Banks	Argentina	Brazil	Mexico	Venezuela	Total	As % of Bank Capital
Citicorp	$1,200	$4,900	$2,900	$1,300	$10,300	160
BankAmerica	425	2,721	2,766	1,508	7,420	145
Manufacturers Hanover	1,293	2,424	1,969	1,083	6,709	206
Chase Manhattan	845	2,830	1,750	1,280	6,705	169
J.P. Morgan	754	1,981	1,228	464	4,427	119
Chemical	373	1,447	1,435	767	4,022	158
Bankers Trust	250	891	1,297	380	2,818	134

Tables 3 and 4 give some idea of the dimensions of the problem. Table 3 shows the foreign indebtedness of selected countries, and the debt as a percentage of each country's GNP, at the end of 1984. Table 4 indicates the exposure of several of the nation's largest banks to four Latin American countries: Argentina, Brazil, Mexico, and Venezuela.

LAISSEZ FAIRE

To cope with this problem, time is needed so that borrowers can be rehabilitated and lending institutions can have the opportunity to charge off loans without further impairing their capital positions. Some claim that this is best accomplished through the free-market process. This group includes the strict disciples of monetarism, who favor not only policies of no official intervention but who also support the lifting of all financial regulations, domestically and internationally.

Free-market monetarists acknowledge that the global financial system would be disrupted if major sovereign debtors should default, but they assert that the disruption will be minor and short-lived. Further, they argue, such dislocation will have its positive aspects, because the disciplinary effect on banks of important overseas losses would produce a healthy reexamination of foreign lending commitments. As a result, bank credit would end up divided more satisfactorily between domestic and foreign markets.

Free-market ideologues are not alone in their adherence to this view. It has a certain fundamental appeal to many groups in the United States. For example, some proponents of lower budget deficits support the argument because such a free-market solution does not require the commitment of additional governmental funds at a time when deficits are already bloated. Critics of commercial banks' activities in this area favor the free-market view because it shifts the burden of adjustment entirely to the banks. Those affected by the credit shortages of recent years perceive the free-market view as leading to more and cheaper credit for domestic use.

OFFICIAL INTERVENTION

Others, however, including myself, believe that the situation is fraught with risk, even from the relatively narrow perspective of the United States. Because bank exposures are so huge (see Table 4), the potential disruption to the system is not small at all, as some continue to insist. Quite the contrary, it is *enormous.* The free-market view would have us wager the heart of the U.S. banking industry on a questionable point made by ideological extremists.

Overcoming the international debt problem requires, among other things, a substantial enlargement of the role of the International Monetary Fund (IMF). The purpose is not to bail out private financial institutions, but rather to prevent the adverse global consequences of defaults and moratoriums—consequences that are not likely to be limited to only a few debtors and creditors.

At the crux of this difficult issue is the role of private financial institutions in international lending and the regulation of those institutions. In the seventies, private lending institutions were saddled with the overwhelming task of intermediating huge transfers of wealth from OPEC to the third world. *Private* institutions were actually encouraged to finance a *political* decision that sprang from weakness in the industrial nations (weakness with respect to energy supplies). In hindsight, it would have been far better if *official* institutions had played a larger role in facilitating this wealth transfer. Private financial institutions would have been stronger—and would be stronger now—and might at least have been willing to finance domestic credit demands at narrower spreads over their cost of funds.

How the United States regulates and supervises its financial institutions and coordinates these monitoring efforts with the authorities in other major countries is one of the most crucial issues of the decade. This is a particularly thorny problem in view of major philosophical differences among the United States, Japan, and European countries regarding how best to control their monetary and credit systems.

In the United States, the Federal Reserve has an arm's-length relationship with the private banking system, and frequently that relationship seems adversarial. The U.S. system is characterized by a relatively large flow of information to the public about the financial health of the banking system and about actions that the regulatory authorities intend to take. In continental Europe, by contrast, the system appears to work on the basis of consensus between the central banks and the governmental institutes of finance, on the one hand, and the major private financial institutions on the other.

Furthermore, in nations other than the United States, details of policy debate and activities of financial institutions are less frequently in the public domain. We do not know, for example, all of the motivations for Western European lending to finance the Soviet Union's gas pipeline, nor do we know the full details of how European banks' claims on Poland and Hungary are being handled. We can be sure, though, that both are the result of an active consensus between the regulators and the regulated.

Assuming that these institutional differences can be overcome, there are two alternative paths that might be followed. One is the further deregulation of financial institutions, and the other is reregulation. With each, there are different philosophical underpinnings and economic and financial consequences.

Supporters of deregulation believe that unrestricted and unfettered financial institutions can better fulfill their intermediary responsibilities for savers and borrowers. It is assumed that the price mechanism—interest rates—will allocate credit efficiently. While this at first appears admirable, because it relies strictly on interest rates in order to keep the market in check, the hidden disciplining force is the willingness to allow financial institutions and debtors of all sizes to fail when the market turns against them.

Overcoming the debt problems of less-developed countries without undue risk all around is too complex and delicate a matter to be left purely to market forces. In the short run, it is essential that time be gained for banks to write off bad international debts under stable market conditions. The longer-term imperative is to develop a regulatory structure and an information flow adequate to cope with the underlying international lending problem. As one aspect of this, the role of the governments of the industrialized countries must be more clearly defined with respect to international lending.

INTERNATIONAL COOPERATION

A coordinated international approach is needed in international lending. Although differences in regulatory philosophy from country to country make such coordination difficult, it is nevertheless crucial. Coordinated prudential rules for bank behavior and for the scope of bank lending should be initiated. Most important, governments—including the United States—should define their commitments to international sovereign lending.

These commitments should be expanded, and sovereigns in the third world should be funded much more by sovereign governments in the industrial world or through official international institutions, such as the IMF and the World Bank. Private commercial banks should continue to make loans that finance the needs of commerce and the investment needs of the private sector.

Key industrial nations also should permit their currencies to become more accessible internationally. This would allow international borrowers to diversify their currency risks and alleviate the hefty burden on the U.S. dollar—a burden that is too heavy considering the U.S. standing in the world economy. International lending is a global responsibility for which all major nations should do their share.

FIXED VERSUS FLOATING EXCHANGE RATES

At the end of World War II, the major trading nations established a system of fixed exchange rates, known as the Bretton Woods system (after Bretton Woods, New Hampshire, where the plans were originally drawn up in 1944). Fixed exchange rates worked fairly well until the early seventies, when they ceased to function due to the strains of an overvalued dollar, chronic U.S. balance of payments deficits, and a persistent drain of gold out of the U.S. Treasury. Since 1973 the leading trading nations have had a floating exchange rate system in which exchange rates fluctuate continuously in response to the pressures of supply and demand.

It was thought at first that floating rates would reduce the overvaluation of the dollar and eliminate the U.S. balance of trade deficits, but obviously this has not happened. If anything, both have gotten worse, not better, so that many responsible governmental and private authorities are now seriously considering a return to fixed exchange rates.

Those who are disenchanted with floating rates claim that if fixed rates had been in existence in recent years they would have provided the policy discipline necessary to prevent the emergence of such large U.S. trade deficits. Those more sympathetic to floating rates scoff at such assertions and ask where the policy discipline was in the sixties, when we had both fixed rates and chronic payments imbalances. They say that such discipline would not have been maintained and that any attempt to revive fixed rates would have been—and is—doomed to failure.

Whichever view one holds, any discussion today of international monetary reform must take into account the profound changes that have occurred in international capital markets in the past dozen years. The Bretton Woods era was basically one of limited international capital mobility. The period of floating rates, by contrast, has been marked by the growing internationalization of capital markets.

For instance, syndicated international bank lending was less than $7 billion in 1972, the last year before the advent of floating exchange rates; in 1985 it was over $50 billion, which is well below the $90 billion peak reached in 1981, just before the onset of the international debt crisis. Eurodeposits outstanding were about $200 million in 1972, about $2.5 billion in 1985. International bond issuance was less than $10 billion in 1972, about $175 billion in 1985. And total private capital inflows into the United States, only $20 billion in 1972, approached $125 billion in 1985.

The internationalization of finance has accelerated in the eighties, even though exchange- and interest-rate volatility have been at all-time highs. This development is particularly striking, since many observers had expected high currency volatility to inhibit international capital mobility. An important reason for this mobility has been the introduction of new financing techniques and instruments to manage exchange-rate and interest-rate risks, including interest-rate and currency swaps and the increased use of both interest-rate and exchange-rate futures and options.

This trend toward greater capital mobility has several important policy implications. More than ever before, capital flows—not trade flows—are now the principal determinant of exchange-rate movements. Moreover, international flows of funds have become increasingly sensitive to interest-rate movements and thus to expectations about future national policy developments that are likely to affect interest rates.

At the same time, the freer flow of capital carries with it an element of risk: the floating exchange-rate system and capital market liberalization have shifted exchange-rate and interest-rate risk away from traditional financial intermediaries and monetary authorities directly to lenders and borrowers. While much recent financial innovation has involved the creation of marketable instruments designed to aid in risk management, these instruments have never really encountered adverse conditions. The transference of risk is not the same thing as reducing the overall amount of risk in the system. The new risk management techniques do not reduce, and may even increase, credit risk.

We are evidently not prepared to accept the discipline of the marketplace with respect to credit creation and capital flows. That discipline implies that lenders and borrowers be exposed to the risk of failure. Recent experience suggests, however, that this is not acceptable in practice. Thus it should be recognized that exchange-rate stabilization would require national monetary authorities to become much more directly involved in managing the credit creation process and in harmonizing regulatory policies affecting financial institutions.

Currently, of course, there are enormous differences among the standards applied by supervisory authorities in different countries to assess such basic criteria as capital adequacy, reserves, and lending and accounting standards. In addition, there are important differences with respect to the activities allowed different kinds of institutions and the degree of public disclosure required of them. In short, the issue of policy coordination is far more complex than is generally acknowledged.

The objective of establishing a more stable exchange-rate environment is a laudable one. Since a return to fixed exchange rates is not realistic in the foreseeable future, the only way to approach the goal is closer supervision and control of the credit creation process worldwide. However, that is easier said than done.

CHAPTER 8

Banking in Changing World Credit Markets

The changing nature of commercial banking, traditionally one of our most staid and conservative industries, has been one of the most startling and dramatic financial developments both domestically and internationally in the last few decades. Not only in the United States, but in most other industrialized nations as well, commercial bank assets and liabilities have grown very rapidly; many innovative services and financing techniques have emerged; competitive pressures have intensified as nonbanks, such as brokerage houses and thrift institutions, have started to offer what are essentially banking services (like checking account facilities and commercial loans); risk taking has increased; and banking practices, policies, and relationships have become far more intricate than they were a generation or so ago.

The pace of these developments is not likely to slow appreciably in the late eighties. Indeed, with deposit-rate ceilings virtually eliminated and interstate banking on the horizon, the pace of change could even accelerate.

BANKING GROWTH

During the past twenty years, say since 1965, commercial banks have grown rapidly in all major countries. The magnitude of this growth has varied with the growth of nominal gross national product and the positioning of banks in the credit structure of their particular country. Commercial bank assets rose during the past twenty years by 11 percent per annum in West Germany, by 14 percent per annum in Canada, 12 percent per annum in Great Britain, 14 percent per annum in Japan, and by 9 percent annually in the United States.

The role of commercial banks is different from country to country with respect to the intermediation of credit. Their market share tends to be higher on the European continent, where "universal" banking is a widely accepted norm, and smaller in the United Kingdom and the United States, where there is a strong division between the activities of commercial banks and those of investment or merchant banks. Thus in Germany banks typically account for about twice as much of the flow of credit to the economy as they do in the United States.

Aside from such differences in institutional structure, instability in world financial markets has changed the role of banks in the credit intermediation process. Rate volatility in the past five years has driven credit demands from the longer-term to the shorter-term markets and has fundamentally altered many nations' saving and investment patterns. In Holland and Germany, for example, where banks have been able to accommodate increased short-term credit demands, their shares have risen, while in Britain, where housing has been a major hedge against inflation and an attractive long-term investment, the involvement of banks in the total flow of credit has diminished.

In the United States, the commercial banks' share of funds supplied to the credit markets has been highly volatile. This has been due to periodic disintermediation because of deposit interest-rate ceilings, the emergence of competing institutions such as money market mutual funds, and other forces. Nevertheless, the role of commercial banks is growing in the American economy as banks respond to invasions into their turf by retaliation in kind. In addition, the diminution in the availability of long-term credit for some corporations in the open credit markets is forcing these borrowers to become increasingly dependent on bank credit.

One often neglected aspect of the growth of American banks in recent decades is their multiplication overseas. In 1960, fewer than a dozen American banks had branches abroad and the assets of those branches added up to less than $5 billion. By 1980, however, nearly two hundred American banks were operating foreign branches and their assets totaled some $400 billion.

In addition to establishing branches abroad, U.S. banks also participate in international financing through Edge Act subsidiaries and International Banking Facilities (IBFs) that are based in the United States but regulated and taxed as though they were located abroad. Edge Act subsidiaries are domestic operations that are engaged strictly in international financing and are given certain legal exemptions that enable them to better compete with foreign banks.

GROWTH OF EUROMARKETS

While the national banking systems in the world are diverse, the Euromarkets are a point of common reference involving the activities of all major banks. The Euromarkets have introduced an element of universality, heretofore unprecedented in banking and finance.

Much of the explosive growth of the Euromarkets (see Table 5) is associated with the intermediation of supplies and demands for foreign exchange, requiring a massive volume of interbank transactions. This function was given substantial impetus when the Bretton Woods system of fixed foreign exchange rates collapsed in 1973 and was replaced by the present system of floating exchange rates, which requires much more trading activity because of the greater degree of uncertainty involved.

Historically, the growth of Euromarkets was also closely associated with the intermediation of the shift in international flows of funds occasioned by the oil price rises of 1973–74 and 1978–79. The surpluses of the Organization of Petroleum Exporting Countries (OPEC) that followed these price hikes led to

Table 5. Growth in Cross-Border Bank Lending to Nonbanks 1973–84 (U.S. Dollars in Billions)

Year	Total Cross-Border Lending	Percent Change
1973	$108.3	36.9
1974	144.1	33.1
1975	172.5	19.7
1976	221.2	28.2
1977	281.5	27.3
1978	363.4	29.1
1979	450.9	24.1
1980	539.9	19.7
1981	645.2	19.5
1982	702.5	8.9
1983	725.1	3.2
1984	735.3	1.4

Source: IMF, International Financial Statistics.

a huge accumulation of Middle Eastern claims on Eurobanks, claims that were intermediated through the Eurobanking system to many developing nations in dire need of funds.

The intermediation functions have not always had smooth sailing. A number of small banks were threatened with insolvency in the wake of the Herstatt crisis in 1974, as depositors threatened to withdraw funds from all but the safest institutions. And in 1977 the central banks of the major economies felt obliged to state publicly that they would act as lenders of last resort to any of their wards whose solvency was threatened by various reschedulings of international claims.

Despite these problems, the major flows of credit through the Euromarkets have been effectively regulated by free-market-like fluctuations in the spreads that sovereign borrowers must pay over the London Interbank Offered Rate (LIBOR). It is difficult to imagine how the credit needs of the less developed countries could possibly have been met in the seventies and early eighties without either the Euromarkets or the banks committed to international banking that comprise the Eurosystem.

The subsequent years—marked by the so-called debt crisis of the developing countries and the large payments imbalances among the major economies—have seen a sharp slowdown in the growth of Eurobank lending. After years of growth rates of 20 percent or more, increases in cross-border bank lending slowed to 3 percent in 1983, and to a mere 1 percent in 1984. At the same time, the international bond markets, and the emerging Note Issuance Facilities, have to a large degree supplanted the role of international bank lending.

Despite the crucial international dimension of the Euromarkets, I cannot help but believe that attention will soon turn from the international features of the markets to the markets' interaction with domestic financial systems in both Europe and the United States. The stocks of Euromarket claims and liabilities are large relative to some comparable domestic magnitudes. Under certain circumstances, Euroclaims are also direct substitutes for bank claims in some domestic markets. As a consequence of this close substitutability, the growth of Euroclaims may threaten the objectives of domestic policy, particularly when the objectives are the control of money or credit.

Eurobank lending and currency operations were for a long while the most spectacular features of the Euromarkets. However, international bond market activity has expanded rapidly. Between 1970 and 1984, international bond markets grew by about 15 percent per year and the total volume outstanding in 1984 was $360 billion. Just as the Eurocredit markets have become substitutes for domestic credit, so the international bond markets have provided alternative sources of longer-term funds for domestic corporations.

BANKING LINKAGES AND INNOVATIONS

Contributing importantly to the growth of banking has been the linking of financial markets, both domestically and internationally, through new financing practices as well as credit instruments. For example, American corporations now arrange bank loans—either syndicated loans or smaller credits from a single bank—that incorporate the option to switch the interest rate from prime-rate-based to LIBOR-based or vice versa on any rollover date, usually every three or six months (see Chart 6).

The U.S. bank prime loan rate tends to be "sticky," often lagging behind open-market rates, especially when interest rates are trending downward. Hence the spread between the prime rate and open-market rates can fluctuate widely, creating an incentive for borrowers to switch to the cheaper alternative on rollover dates.

The crucial point from a U.S. credit flow analysis perspective is that when a customer chooses the prime-based option, an American bank is likely to book the loan domestically and report it to the Federal Reserve as a domestic loan. Conversely, if a customer chooses LIBOR-based pricing, the loan often will be

Financial Markets

Chart 6. U.S. Bank Prime Rate and London LIBOR, 1977–85

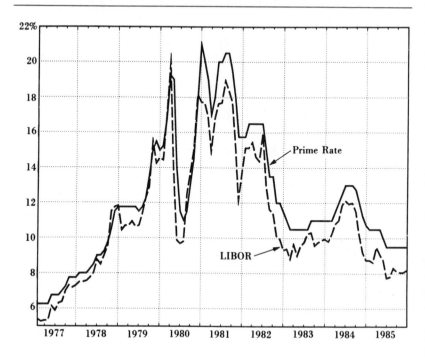

booked in an offshore branch of the same U.S. bank. In this case, the loan will not show up in the regular domestic bank lending statistics, which means that domestic bank credit data may occasionally distort the true picture of U.S. corporate credit demands.

Another striking aspect of international financial transactions is their increasing level of sophistication. A series of transactions by the World Bank early in the eighties illustrates the point. As a matter of policy, the World Bank tends to borrow in low-interest-rate markets, because the interest rate it charges less-developed-country borrowers is based on an average of the World Bank's cost of capital, excluding currency fluctuations.

Therefore, in recent years, World Bank borrowings have been

heavily concentrated in currencies such as Swiss francs and deutsche marks and Japanese yen, and investors in those markets have substantial holdings of World Bank bonds. Moreover, issuance in the Swiss franc market involves some delay, as there is an officially regulated queue, and at the time these transactions took place in Germany the authorities were keen to limit foreign bond issuance as a means of holding down capital outflows. Conversely, World Bank debt has been a rarity in higher-interest-rate countries.

With this background, the World Bank found it attractive to create, in effect, some Swiss franc and deutsche mark liabilities, with the help of its investment bankers. The innovative financing procedure was as follows. First, a bond was issued in the Eurodollar market, then the dollar proceeds from this issue were swapped into deutsche marks and Swiss francs via a long-term foreign exchange contract. Thus, a dollar liability was converted into a liability in these two other currencies. As an added bonus, the all-in cost—the Eurodollar bond interest rate and the currency swap premium—was less than the cost of a direct borrowing in the deutsche mark or Swiss franc markets. The entire transaction was completed within a matter of days, since there was no need to wait in either the German or Swiss issuing queues. (As of May 1985, the German authorities have eliminated the queuing system for issuance of Euro-Deutschemark bonds.)

Hedged transactions are also increasingly important in international money markets. For example, many investors routinely compare the return in hedged Canadian dollar instruments with that in comparable U.S. dollar instruments, placing their funds with the highest return. Without a doubt, one of the important trends of the eighties is the inclination and ability of international money market participants to create custom-tailored synthetic vehicles, by combining instruments denominated in one currency with foreign exchange swaps or contracts, or even interest-rate futures.

Although swap markets have been growing for a number of

years, it is generally agreed that there was a dramatic increase in the volume of transactions of both interest-rate and currency swaps in 1984. Swaps allow the particularly fine terms that may be available to a specific borrower in a specific market to be transferred to other markets. These markets have been broadened to include a greater variety of participants and have moved beyond simple counterparty transactions to a more standardized trading format. One of the factors driving the growth of this market has been the desire of financial institutions, such as the World Bank and other major capital market participants, to diversify the currencies in which they borrow. They have been able to utilize the swap market on many occasions to obtain their preferred currency exposure on more favorable terms than would have been possible by directly issuing debt denominated in that currency.

THE FREEING OF MARKETS

To some extent, financial innovation was stimulated by banking regulations that inhibited the growth of traditional banking. These constraints contributed to the burgeoning Euromarkets, to a number of new financial centers, and to the introduction of new credit instruments. In recent years, however, the philosophy of financial deregulation has been in the saddle worldwide. As a result, credit market barriers among institutions and among countries have been partially dismantled on the premise that the most efficient way to allocate funds domestically is by the price of money and internationally by freely floating exchange rates.

Although deregulation has made its greatest strides in the United States, similar tendencies are also evident elsewhere. For example, Britain removed foreign exchange controls, which had been in existence for many years. Pressures for British deregulation have also yielded similar results in the banking industry and elsewhere; major liberalization takes effect in 1986 in the gilt-edge bond market and the stock exchange.

The trend to deregulation is even apparent in such tradition-ally structured and controlled economies as Japan. Domestically, competitive interbank markets in call money have been allowed to develop, as well as an active retail market in yen CDs. Foreign exchange controls have been relaxed and many Japanese insur-ance companies and pension funds—like their brethren in the United States and the United Kingdom—are diversifying some assets into international markets.

Table 6 provides summary information on current bank regu-lation and competition in six major foreign industrial countries.

The full effects of financial deregulation have yet to be felt in the United States. The impact is likely to be diverse. With the advent of many new kinds of deposits carrying market interest rates, disintermediation may be a phenomenon of the past.

When disintermediation gripped American financial markets in the past, depositors withdrew funds to invest in marketable credit obligations of the U.S. Government and municipalities and of higher-rated business corporations. Lower-quality bor-rowers were thereby shut out from access to funds. In the ab-sence of disintermediation, the credit-rationing process will not occur as quickly. However, it will take place at a much higher level of interest rates—namely, when financing costs become an oppressive component of doing business. With a delay, there-fore, businesses with limited financing alternatives will still be rationed out of the credit markets, but they may be left in a more vulnerable liability position than previously.

Financial deregulation is also likely to encourage commercial banks to become more oriented to domestic rather than interna-tional lending. This, on balance, will benefit corporate finance in the United States. In other words, financial regulation, which circumscribed banking activity in the United States, probably induced banks to enlarge their role internationally (because foreign branches could escape restrictive domestic regulation).

Today, the poor experience with much international lending, the huge volume of outstanding foreign loans, and the liberaliza-

Table 6. Current Regulatory and Competitive Conditions for Banks, Selected Foreign Industrial Countries

| Country | Regulation | | Competition | |
	Interest-rate Controls	Balance-sheet Constraints	Other Financial Institutions	Nonbank Financial Assets
Canada	No (ceilings on certain certificate of deposit rates, 1972–75)	No	Trust and mortgage loan companies, credit unions, insurance companies	Government bonds
France	Yes (ceilings except for long-term, large-denomination time deposits)	Credit expansion ceilings (officially lifted 1985)	Savings banks	Government bonds, bond funds
Germany	No	No	Life insurance companies	Small-denomination government bonds
Italy	No	Credit expansion ceilings (officially lifted 1983)	Savings banks, special credit institutions	Treasury bills
Japan	Yes (regulated except for foreign currency deposits and certificates of deposit)	Window guidance (limits on bank lending)	Postal savings	Bond funds
United Kingdom	No (not since 1975)	No (limits on growth of interest-bearing liabilities, intermittently 1973–80)	Building societies	Government-issued national savings certificates, money market funds

Source: Federal Reserve *Bulletin* (October 1985).

100

tion of the domestic banking scene are encouraging banks to become more active domestically.

The trend of commercial banks, therefore, is taking a strange turn. The regulations prevailing during the sixties and seventies contributed toward an outward search for growth, the massive increase in debt of less developed countries, and the overextension of international credit. In contrast, the deregulation of financial institutions is now turning bank lending inward and limiting the availability of funds internationally, where the need for credit remains urgent.

CHAPTER 9

The Equity Market over the Long Term

A dynamic, healthy equity market—one in which new capital can be raised and in which investors are provided reasonable marketability—is essential for the survival of capitalism and for a democratic economic society. Risk capital is the cornerstone of a free economy. It stands for freedom of economic choice and for economic efficiency and growth achieved through profit incentives.

Growth of equity in the form of retained profits is a major savings mechanism as well as the capital allocation system of modern market economies. The capacity to borrow rests on the foundation of equity capital. Without sufficient equity, private money and bond markets could not function. Indeed, weakness in the capital base is often the forerunner of credit quality deterioration and, ultimately, of economic stagnation.

GROWTH OF THE EQUITY MARKET

Historically, over the long haul, increases in the total market value of equities have generally paralleled the growth of nominal gross national product (GNP). However, although it used to be the conventional view that inflation was good for stock prices, the experience of the past quarter century indicates otherwise: equity markets do best in an environment of balanced economic growth and do not benefit from long periods of accelerating inflation. As noted earlier, the double-digit inflationary episodes of the seventies and early eighties revealed that stocks are not as good a hedge against inflation as had been thought.

In the model world of econometrics—the sort of world that many economists find unduly attractive—relative relationships are supposed to remain the same when the nominal value of everything goes up. In other words, the value of corporate equity is supposed to climb at the same rate as nominal productive capacity, which in turn tracks the rise of nominal GNP. Of course this has not been the case in the United States in the past quarter century. Productivity gains expected from new plant and equipment were vitiated by high energy costs and the high cost of environmental-protection equipment. Inflation did not burden corporate income and cost statements evenly. In many industries, cost inflation raced ahead of price increases, so that what has been called the "inflation flow-through" never really occurred.

The result was an inability to finance growth through retained profits, leading to a massive explosion of debt that hurt the equity market. From the early fifties to the mid-sixties, outstanding credit market debt—the liabilities of government, business, and households—exceeded the total market value of equities by a ratio of 2:1 (see Chart 5, page 40). Subsequently, the ratio deteriorated until it reached 3½:1 at the end of 1984.

Policy-makers and businessmen should not delude themselves into believing that corporations will be able to pass on the cost of rampant inflation, should it reoccur; the social structure in major industrial countries will no longer permit such a pass-through. Fortunately, inflation will remain only a cyclical phenomenon, at least for the time being. The scars are still tender and deep, and a new wave of high inflation cannot easily be triggered in a world with large debt, hesitant lenders, and a financial market that responds promptly and adversely to inflationary developments.

During the next few decades, the equity market will also have to contend with intensified competition from the debt market. In an era of financial deregulation, marketable debt instruments are in the forefront of innovation—including novel features with respect to maturity, floating or fixed coupons, tax aspects, collateralization, as well as other terms. Portfolio managers have an ever-widening choice of alternatives and even small sums can now be invested at market interest rates in a variety of securities that were not even imagined only a decade ago.

The interest-rate structure that is emerging will hamper business corporations and therefore equities. In a deregulated financial system very low interest rates will occur infrequently, and perhaps only in times of extreme economic distress, because interest rates have become a major means of economic discipline. Virtually all savers are now paid market interest rates whereas previously the below-market rates paid to many savers benefited borrowers, including corporations, to the extent that they leveraged their capital positions.

Negative, or very small positive, real after-tax interest costs, a regular feature of yesterday's economic environment, are now a thing of the past. In addition, lenders now require higher risk premia to compensate for greater market volatility, additionally complicating the task of initiating new borrowings.

THE EMERGING GLOBAL EQUITY MARKET

Despite competition from the proliferation of new debt instruments, the equity market not only will continue to expand but will become more international. Considerable progress has already been made in establishing global equity markets; the size of major equity markets around the world has grown and trading linkages have improved.

Eventually, around-the-clock equity trading will become common. Already some stocks trade almost around the clock on listed exchanges around the world. Sony Corporation shares, for example, are traded from 9:30 A.M. to 4 P.M. in New York and until 4:30 P.M. on the Pacific Exchange. The shares then open at 8 P.M. (New York time) in Tokyo and are traded until 10 P.M.; they resume between 12 A.M. to 2 A.M. Two hours later, at 4 A.M. (New York time), Sony shares trade again when the exchanges open in Paris, Amsterdam, Frankfurt, Munich, and London.

The rationale for the development of global equity markets is compelling. First, studies have shown that investors can achieve less volatility of return by diversifying internationally. Second, the expanding international activity of business corporations is gradually increasing the number of companies with stocks that are traded on more than one national market. And third, the information gap—a key barrier to the internationalization of equity markets—is narrowing.

Contributing to the internationalization of the equity market, as well as to its changing character in general, are vast improvements taking place in communications. Just a few years ago, most financial data was available only in printed form. Now the trend is moving rapidly toward making information accessible in readily usable computerized form, already linked into powerful analytical programs.

For example, using the Salomon Brothers STOCKFACTS system, it is possible in about two minutes to select a group of companies, prepare a complete set of merged financial state-

105

ments (weighted in any proportion), develop financial ratios for the composite, and obtain a graphic comparison between that group and any other group.

Soon companies will transmit quarterly and annual reports directly into one or more centralized data bases. Subscribers will be able to plug the new numbers directly into their financial models of these companies, as well as into their valuation and portfolio models. Another revolutionary change is occurring with respect to communicating information from dealers to investors. Market information and analyses can be transmitted by direct broker-to-client hookups through CRT screens and computers; traditional industry or company analyses can be scanned by users in summary form through video screens and then retrieved in complete form through printouts only when needed.

Trading procedures and decision-making patterns are also affected by the communications revolution that is taking place. Some bond traders scan as many as eight screens simultaneously, screens that display prices and yield spreads or that show interactive computations. However, responsibility for a trade still falls on an individual who does not have an unlimited capacity to absorb information. In other words, the processing of information is as important as its delivery. To make large and rapid flows of information quickly comprehensible to traders, communications channels will have to interpret as well as display.

THE GROWTH OF PROXY INSTRUMENTS

Another important dynamic within the securities market is the development of various types of proxy instruments such as options, index futures, options on futures, and options on indexes for cash settlement. The United States is in the vanguard of this area of innovation, but undoubtedly these proxies will proliferate in other markets around the world.

This part of the market has expanded rapidly. In the United States, there are at this writing five index futures contracts, eight different options on cash settlement indexes, and two options on index futures, all of which trade on two exchanges. Additional futures contracts have been approved but are not yet being traded. There are more than twenty stock index futures pending approval and more than a dozen nonstock index futures have been proposed, including the consumer price index, housing starts, additional currencies, and metals indexes.

Some data on the magnitude of a few of these proxy instruments are informative. The average daily volume on the New York Stock Exchange in 1984 was $3 billion, while the underlying value of the stock futures contracts, consisting of the Standard & Poor's 500 and New York Stock Exchange futures, averaged $3.7 billion. Put and call options trading averaged 180,000 contracts per day, and trading in options on indexes is off to a very good start.

In the market for U.S. Government securities in 1984, the daily volume of transactions in bonds with a maturity of more than ten years averaged $6.1 billion, compared with $4.5 billion in Treasury bond futures.

The futures markets in all major currencies are also growing rapidly. In the United States, futures markets in five key currencies experienced a daily average trading volume of $2.7 billion in 1984. While still modest, the growth has been enormous since only $860 million at the beginning of 1980. Options trading in currencies and fixed-income securities is also gaining momentum at a rapid pace.

There are opposing views on the merits of proxy instruments. Some assert that they lower the cost of trading primary securities, that they only transfer a small volume of funds away from the cash market, and that they decrease the variability of returns and lower the risks for market makers. Others claim that these proxies divert savings from long-term investments, increase market volatility, overemphasize short-term investment per-

107

formance, and add a speculative element to the serious business of channeling savings to investments. However this discussion is resolved, proxy securities have come too far to disappear; there is no doubt that they will continue to be a major new dimension in world markets.

THE EXPANDING ROLE OF THE INSTITUTIONAL INVESTOR

The institutionalization of the market has been striking. Institutional investors, both in the United States and abroad, now hold about 44 percent of the market value of U.S. stocks as compared with only about 10 percent in 1950. Block trades—trades of 10,000 or more shares—now account for 51 percent of all trades on the New York Stock Exchange, approximately double the percentage of the late seventies.

These trends are likely to persist. The institutional component of the equity market may well reach the 65 percent to 70 percent level within a few decades. The financial intermediation process is highly efficient. While the flow of savings into contractual savings institutions, such as pension funds and insurance companies, will continue to be large, it may not climb at the rapid pace of recent decades because of the pressure by corporations to slow pension contributions.

More savings will probably be allocated to institutions on a discretionary basis. Many households will have the opportunity, through computer and financial technology, to shift their savings among financial institutions virtually at will. They will be able to move funds in and out of groupings of equities and fixed-income obligations. Mutual funds should benefit from the continued institutionalization of the market, because they have low overhead and can be structured to fulfill many specialized investment objectives; eventually, this will include the use of futures and options in strategic decisions.

While institutional investors will continue to dominate the

equity market, "boutique" portfolio management groups will still proliferate. Typically, exceptionally able portfolio managers attempt to maximize their own profits, which in the management of stocks and bonds entails little overhead and offers a highly leveraged potential reward. Investors also seek out such managers because of the increasing absolute number of stocks and because of the belief that higher returns are found by investing in smaller companies.

Investment boutiques will also benefit from the ongoing belief that they are able to achieve superior results because they have relatively modest-sized portfolios and have greater flexibility in decision making. If this were true, superior performance could be achieved by making all institutional portfolios small. The fact remains that investors, whether in bonds or stocks, cannot escape from the performance of the general economy; eventually, they are either helped or hurt by it.

A MORE DEMANDING ROLE FOR SECURITIES DEALERS

Within this new setting, securities dealers will be greatly affected in a number of ways.

1. While trading volume will mushroom in the coming decades, comparable gains in dealer profits are not ensured. The deregulation of financial markets will attract new brokers and market-making participants, which is bound to reduce profit margins. Furthermore, technical support to facilitate transactions will boost overhead costs significantly.

2. Around-the-clock trading in stocks and bonds will intensify dealer activity. Dealers will be required to be much more involved in international currency markets and in limiting volatility risks.

3. The institutionalization of the equity market will enhance the market-making function of dealers, because New York Stock Exchange specialists do not have the capital or the distribution facilities to complete large trades.

4. Large equity trades will necessitate strong dealer capability in fixed-income securities, because with a stronger emphasis on total rate of return, investors are bound to want to shift periodically from bonds to stocks and vice versa.

5. The capital requirements of securities dealers will accelerate rapidly, resulting in further industry consolidation or mergers with financial institutions having access to capital. Making markets for blocks of stocks and bonds will enlarge dealers' positions. Moreover, most market makers are likely to be active in a variety of securities, both domestic and international, which will also magnify their capital needs.

6. Maintaining effective control and correctly judging risks and rewards will be a difficult task for securities dealers. Their balance sheets will be filled with hedging and arbitraging transactions involving traditional and new proxy securities in domestic and international markets, all of which will be activated by aggressive young trading specialists whose historical view of risks and rewards is likely to be overwhelmed by the potential for profit and quick success.

NEW CHALLENGES FOR INVESTMENT DECISION MAKERS

Like it or not, investment decisions will undergo greater scrutiny and face new types of challenges in the future. The shift away from traditional smokestack industries and toward service industries, with the accompanying reduced status of physical assets, calls for improvements in analytical judgments. It is much easier to draw conclusions about a business with large natural and physical resources than one in which labor and management dominate. Human capital, technical expertise, and scientific training are bound to play key roles in the emerging financial world.

Evaluating these will be difficult; they do not have assembly-line characteristics; they will encourage management and skill transfers among firms or, alternatively, the formation of new enterprises; and it is more difficult for such firms to plow back large amounts of earnings. As a result, size alone may not produce the efficiency once contained in large manufacturing entities. Some of the more successful firms may be of moderate size and, consequently, too small for broad public ownership.

The greater challenge to the investment decision maker, however, will emanate from the spawning of new marketable securities and security proxies. This will produce even more intensive comparisons between the total rate of return on stocks and the performance of various fixed-income securities. Furthermore, these comparisons will be made over shorter time spans, because investors tend to be risk averse and get somewhat shortsighted and because portfolio managers compete aggressively to manage funds. These developments are likely to accentuate volatility in the price behavior of securities. The growth and popularity of marketable credit instruments contribute to the volatility of prices because the performance of the obligation is measurable. Nonmarketable obligations, on the other hand, have as their main feature a commitment of funds for a specific maturity that cannot be changed.

In view of the likely growth of many tradable obligations, one should recall the caution sounded by John Maynard Keynes in his famous chapter "The State of Long-term Expectation" in *The General Theory of Employment, Interest and Money* (1936): "As the organization of investment markets improves," he wrote, "the risk of the predominance of speculation increase(s)." He further noted that when investment markets are organized with

111

a view toward liquidity, "the professional investor is forced to concern himself with the anticipation of impending changes, in the news or in the atmosphere, of the kind by which experience shows that the mass psychology of the market is most influenced."

Additionally, Keynes added, "Of the maxims of orthodox finance none, surely, is more anti-social than the fetish of liquidity. . . . It forgets that there is no such thing as liquidity of investment for the community as a whole. The social object of skilled investment should be to defeat the dark forces of time and ignorance which envelop our future. The actual, private object of the most skilled investment today is to 'beat the gun,' as the Americans so well express it, to outwit the crowd, and to pass the bad, or depreciating, half-crown to the other fellow."

While these cautions may be dramatic, they are well worth remembering in this changing world of financial innovations, deregulation, global trading, and a rising volume of marketable securities, all of which combine to create an illusion of liquidity. These developments will provide great opportunities as long as those involved in financial markets recognize that they are not running casinos but rather organizations that should help channel funds to the most productive and efficient economic uses.

CHAPTER 10

Fallen Financial Dogmas and Beliefs

Gone are the regular ebbs and flows of financial transactions, the almost predictable market oscillations that once accompanied business cycles. Gone, too, are many of the rules, regulations, and traditions that in the past produced certain acceptable market practices and conservative standards of prudent financial behavior.

It should come as no surprise, therefore, to find that important financial dogmas have fallen and that many traditional beliefs have been uprooted. With these changes, we have lost many analytical groundings that were once used as guides for financial decisions. This chapter discusses seven of these dogmas and beliefs, the reasons for their fall, and the implications of the resulting discontinuities.

1. *High real interest rates encourage substantial increases in savings.*

This dogma was resurrected by supply-side economists in the early eighties (although it had previously been questioned by Keynesians who viewed income, rather than interest rates, as the main determinant of savings). The forceful rhetoric of supply siders garnered considerable support for this tenet, but it has disappointed its adherents because savings have *not* grown substantially in response to the extraordinarily high real interest rates of recent years (see Chart 7).

For example, real interest rates—as measured by the differen-

Chart 7. Savings Rate versus Inflation-Adjusted Interest Rates, 1960–85

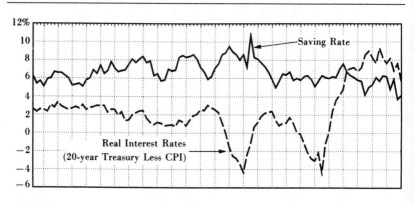

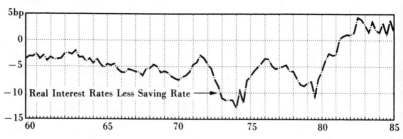

tial between yields on long-term Government bonds and the rate of increase in consumer prices—averaged about 5 percent during the five years from the beginning of 1980 through the end of 1984. This compares with a real interest rate approximating zero in the immediately preceding five-year period. But saving as a percentage of disposable income averaged only 6 percent in 1980–84, slightly *less* than the 7 percent that prevailed during the preceding five years.

Clearly, large changes in the savings ratio must be influenced by factors other than interest-rate inducements. These factors may include unexpected economic or political shocks, sharp changes in inflationary expectations, uncertainty about the future, or other developments.

2. *High real interest rates discourage economic recovery.*

Like the first one, this dogma appears incontrovertible on the surface. Indeed, ten or twenty years ago predictions of a weak economy would have abounded in circumstances characterized by real interest rates as high as those that prevailed during the years 1980–84 (see Chart 8). Several factors have changed, however, thus invalidating this traditional belief.

First, the restrictive effects of interest rates on business activity have been diluted both by financial deregulation and by innovation. The combination of these two developments has increased income for households, thus strengthening their capacity to borrow. More importantly, because of the proliferation of new financing techniques, borrowers have been able to avoid being locked into the high-fixed-rate, long-term market. Both business and households now borrow heavily at interest rates that are tied in some way to money market rates, while the long-term fixed-rate market has come to be dominated by the federal, state, and local governments.

With a positively sloped yield curve—that is, a typically normal-shaped yield curve, wherein short-term rates are lower than long-term rates—the initial financing cost in the short

115

Chart 8. Real GNP Growth versus Inflation-Adjusted Interest Rates, 1960–85

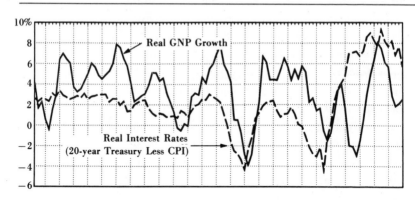

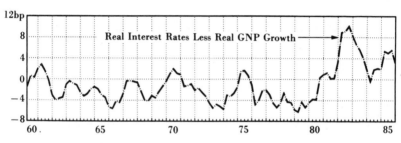

market is a powerful inducement to finance short. To be sure, the borrower assumes the risk that interest rates could rise in the future, but nevertheless he can take comfort from the historical record that yield inversions (short rates higher than long) occur infrequently and typically do not last long. There is also the common belief, right or wrong, that because real interest rates are so high they are bound to decline, so that by financing short or through floating-rate vehicles the benefits of the expected fall in rates will quickly accrue to the borrower.

3. Financial deregulation lowers the general level of interest rates.
This belief is rooted in the assumption that the competition fostered by deregulation will drive interest rates down in the

same way that deregulation has tended to lower some prices in commerce and industry. The analogy, however, is faulty. The reduction of prices in industry reflects new entrants increasing the supply of goods and services.

In contrast, interest rates are determined by the overall demand and supply of credit. The supply of credit, however, is determined by the Federal Reserve, not by the private sector. A financial intermediary competing in a newly deregulated market will have an initial downward influence on interest rates in that market. But shifting its resources to the new market implies reducing its participation in other arenas, where rates will be affected in the opposite direction.

Of course, in a highly deregulated market a financial intermediary may not be satisfied with merely *shifting* its resources from one market to another. More likely, it will choose to *enlarge* its total role. Thus it will become more aggressive in competing for resources, thereby generally elevating the cost of liabilities to all financial intermediaries. This result becomes especially pronounced when institutions with insured deposits are involved, because they can aggressively bid for funds without depositors scrutinizing their credit practices.

Financial deregulation has also encouraged floating-rate financing, which has tended to exacerbate cyclical swings in interest rates. As already noted in earlier chapters, floating-rate financing allows intermediaries to quickly pass on their cost of funds to final borrowers. By removing the traditional interest-rate risk from financial intermediation, intermediaries are no longer inhibited in their lending by rising rates. In such an environment, intermediary profits depend mainly on *increasing* their assets and liabilities, so that intermediaries are not part of the restraining mechanism when the central bank limits reserve availability. In fact, since the intermediary is not inhibited by monetary restraint, it is able, through the floating-rate process, to actually *oppose* the Fed's efforts.

In sum, financial deregulation does not lower interest rates

117

generally; rather, it has the following implications. First, it brings uniformity to different interest rates. Local and regional sources of funds are now subject to the bidding of the U.S. and international money markets. Second, it raises the cost of funds to financial intermediaries as they attempt to enlarge the scope of their activities. Third, the advent of floating rates and the elimination of interest-rate ceilings permit intermediaries to escape the direct discipline of rising interest rates. As a result, when restraint is necessary the central bank is required to exert even greater market pressure than before.

4. *Credit quality is constant in our financial system.*

This belief used to be deeply imbedded in the marketplace. In the twenty years following World War II, it was a bedrock attribute of our credit markets: business cycle swings were moderate, financial practices were tempered and moderated by lingering memories of the Great Depression, and double-digit inflation was not yet destabilizing the economy. Today, we recognize that financial practices, balance-sheet strategies, and portfolio behavior have, in the past decade or two, been pushed toward the outer limits of safety with regard to the preservation of capital. Even the credit instruments of the highest rated business corporations and financial institutions do not bear the standard of credit quality that was theirs in earlier periods. Indeed, now there are fewer such high-quality entities around.

Today, only one major U.S. bank is AAA-rated. In 1974, 81 percent of all outstanding publicly offered corporate bonds had ratings of A or better. At present, this has dipped below 70 percent. In addition, households have demonstrated a willingness to commit an increasing proportion of their income to service borrowings. Against this backdrop, no large business firm or financial institution can withstand the corroding influence of loose financial practices and a general swing toward credit deterioration.

No one now can clearly estimate the bounds of safety and

danger in this break with constancy in credit quality. From a long-term point of view, the management, supervision, and regulation of financial markets and institutions are in transition: they are headed toward further deregulation and then, ultimately, to some new forms of reregulation and/or closer supervision.

5. *The growth of debt is closely linked to growth in nominal gross national product.*

The breaking of the close link between debt and economic activity is dramatically illustrated in Chart 9. The proliferation of debt is actually understated in Chart 9, because the available data do not fully capture many new contingent liabilities such as interest-rate and currency swaps, the use of options and futures, and off-balance-sheet financing techniques like standby letters of credit. (On the same subject, also see Chart 3, page 36.)

6. *A nation's large trade deficit weakens its currency in foreign exchange markets.*

This well-entrenched dogma, which has been overturned in recent years, had gained credence both by economic theory and by historical evidence. Exchange rates are supposed to adjust, over time, in order to narrow both trade and current account imbalances. Indeed, for most of the era since World War II there was a fairly high correlation between a nation's deficit on current account and depreciation of its currency.

As Chart 10 shows, however, this relationship has been breached in the last few years, at least insofar as the dollar is concerned. As U.S. current account deficits have mounted, the dollar has *strengthened,* not weakened, reflecting a flight of capital from abroad to the United States.

A strong demand for dollars by foreigners, combined with a sizable contraction in the lending of dollars to foreign borrowers, rocketed the dollar upward in foreign currency markets. The result has been an increase in U.S. imports (because foreign

Chart 9. Domestic Nonfinancial Sectors—Outstanding Debt as a Percentage of Nominal Gross National Product, 1965–85

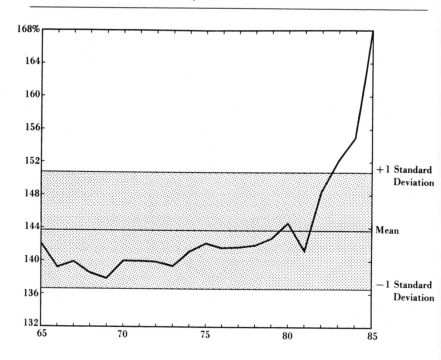

goods and services are cheaper for Americans, who get more foreign money for a dollar) and a decrease in U.S. exports (because American goods and services are more expensive for foreigners, who have to pay more of their own money to get a dollar). Once and for all, this has demonstrated the dynamism of capital flows and how they can alter trade relationships.

These capital flows were encouraged by important fundamentals that favored investment in the United States. One of the factors giving the United States a comparative advantage has been a more innovative and deregulated financial system than those prevailing elsewhere. Deregulation and innovation have permitted the U.S. economy to expand even in the face of high

120

Chart 10. Trade-Weighted Dollar versus the Current Account Balance and Net Private Capital Inflows, 1974–84 (Dollars in Billions)

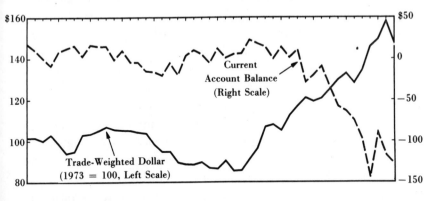

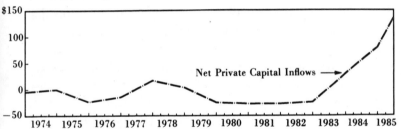

real interest rates, as noted above. Both have also contributed to the creation of new financing techniques, new credit instruments, and, thus, new investment opportunities that have facilitated and encouraged the flow of money to the United States.

American corporations borrow globally in U.S. dollars. The U.S. Treasury tailors its obligation to appeal to foreign accounts. U.S. mortgages are marketed abroad in securitized form. Domestic debt obligations, supported by options and futures, offer wide-ranging opportunities along the entire yield curve—far beyond anything available outside the United States.

Other major nations, however, are now in the process of deregulating *their* credit markets, and if this trend continues, it

121

will have profound implications for future capital flows. If the gap in deregulation between the United States and other key financial markets around the world were to narrow substantially, capital flows will become even more powerful in determining foreign exchange values. The reason is that many more opportunities than now exist will become available to attract funds quickly across national borders. This responsiveness will be speeded along by transactions in marketable obligations that are executed quickly in response to changing economic and financial expectations in a world where massive information-gathering capabilities and near-term interpretive analysis will intensify volatility in foreign exchange and domestic financial markets.

Moreover, when the U.S. dollar weakens, as is ultimately highly likely, the more deregulated financial systems in other major industrial nations will increase the magnitude of the dollar's decline. The new and highly diversified opportunities abroad will be a powerful magnet in attracting funds *from* the United States, in the same way that varied investment opportunities have facilitated the flow of funds *into* the United States. Thus capital flows, as opposed to trade flows, will become fully established as the major determinant of foreign exchange values.

7. *Fiscal policy can be a flexible anticyclical tool and, combined with monetary policy, can prolong economic expansion and limit economic and financial excesses.*

Stemming from John Maynard Keynes, this belief gained momentum in the early sixties as a result of three factors:

1. President John F. Kennedy lowered taxes and successfully stimulated economic recovery.
2. Cyclical swings in the economy in the first three decades following World War II were rather mild.
3. The rhetoric of some economists suggested that we had entered a new era, an era of fine-tuning, wherein flexible

compensatory fiscal measures could be used to effect soft landings, apply midcourse corrections and make rolling readjustments.

But swings from budget deficits in recessions to surpluses in economic booms never materialized. Largely because of political factors, we get deficits in recessions but fail to get surpluses in booms; we just get slightly smaller deficits. A massive structural deficit now confronts the United States, meaning that even at high employment we have a large built-in budget deficit given present tax rates and spending programs. The best that can be hoped for now is a gradual reduction in that deficit instead of a fiscal policy that responds quickly to changing economic conditions.

Lack of a flexible fiscal policy will continue to have important ramifications for American financial markets. As in recent years, it leaves the burden of stabilization mainly to monetary policy. In a deregulated and innovative marketplace, though, monetary policy will have to drive interest rates harder and higher when restraint is required and when no help is forthcoming from the fiscal side (indeed, quite the opposite). Markets will also be more volatile because market participants, aware of the dominant role of the central bank, will therefore anticipate and scrutinize its actions all the more closely in the absence of fiscal flexibility.

PART III

Interest Rates

CHAPTER 11

Secular and Cyclical Trends in Interest Rates

Interest rates are the product of financial transactions, the prices paid by borrowers and sellers of securities and received by lenders and buyers of securities for the short- and long-term use of money. This chapter and the three following ones are devoted to the behavior of interest rates because they play such a key role in investment and portfolio decision making.

SECULAR TRENDS

Secular patterns encompass long periods of time, many decades perhaps, during which interest rates basically sweep upward or downward. These broad movements are clearly discernible even

127

though they may be interrupted by cyclical movements from time to time, with the cyclical fluctuations ranging from less than a year to several years in length.

Chart 11, based on the pioneering work of Sidney Homer, illustrates broad secular trends in long-term interest rates since 1800, and Table 7 gives further details covering roughly the same period.

Chart 11 and Table 7 show that secular trends overwhelm cyclical patterns. There have been five secular bear bond markets since 1800 and five bull bond markets. *Bear bond markets* are periods of *rising interest rates;* they take their name from the falling bond prices that accompany the rising rates. Similarly,

Chart 11. Long-Term High-Grade U.S. Bonds, 1800–1985 (Annual Averages)

Table 7. Secular Swings in Long-Term American Interest Rates

| | *Annual Average Yields* | | | *Change* | | *Duration* |
	Peak %	*Trough* %	*Peak* %	*In Basis Points*	*In Percentage*	*in Years*
Governments:						
1798	7.56					
1810		5.82		−174	−23	12
1814			7.64	+182	+31	4
				+ 8		16
1814	7.64					
1824		4.25		−339	−44	10
1842			6.07	+182	+43	18
				−157		28
1842	6.07					
1853		4.02		−205	−34	11
1861			6.45	+243	+61	8
				+ 38		19
1861	6.45					
Corporates:						
1899		3.20		−325	−49	38
1920			5.27	+207	+65	21
				−118		59
1920	5.27					
1946		2.45		−282	−54	26
1981			13.57	+1112	+454	35
				+ 830		61

bull markets are periods of rising bond prices but *falling interest rates.* Some have endured for as little as four years, early in our history, and others for many decades.

As Table 7 indicates, the magnitude of the interest-rate movements from peak to trough or vice versa ranged from 23 percent to 54 percent in secular bull markets (falling rates), and from 31 percent to 65 percent in bear markets (rising rates) prior to the last secular bear market that started in 1946.

It is significant to examine this astonishing secular bear market that began in 1946 against the backdrop of what happened earlier in the present century. From 1900 to 1920, a bear market was in force that raised long-term interest rates by 65 percent from trough to peak (see Table 7). This was followed by a secular bull market from 1920 to 1946, during which long rates fell by 54 percent. Then began the greatest rate upsweep in our history—it has endured for at least 35 years thus far (that is, through 1981) and, as Table 7 indicates, has raised long rates by 454 percent.

We do not yet know whether this great secular bear market has ended. In the last cyclical upward push, new secular highs were recorded in October 1981. Thereafter, rates have fallen cyclically, but there is not yet evidence that we have entered a *secular* period of declining rates. An important test is ahead for this most tenacious and vibrant secular bear market in history.

Correctly assessing a shift in the secular direction of interest rates is by far the most complex feat in interest-rate forecasting. There is nothing that is more complicated and difficult to evaluate in all of investment and portfolio analysis. Rising rates have often been associated with wars, such as the Civil War and World War I, and roughly with rising inflation; falling rates, on the other hand, have been correlated with longer periods of reasonable economic stability as well as with depressions and deflation.

But that is far from the whole story. There are many additional elements involved, including changes in financial regulation, economic stabilization policies, expectations, financial innovation, and international financial linkages. Making judgments on a change in the secular trend of interest rates is like standing in the middle of a block trying to estimate what is coming around the corner. Even so, market participants who focus entirely on cyclical elements—which is the typical way of going about things—and ignore secular rate trends, do so at their peril.

Despite the hazards, I want to explore whether the great secular rise in interest rates that began in 1946 has finally run its course. The developments suggesting that it has include, first of all, the sharp decline in the rate of inflation that has taken place in the United States and in other key industrial nations. In addition, credit growth outside the United States has slowed substantially, particularly in the developing countries that are now handicapped by a large debt burden. Most industrial nations are also now pursuing only moderately stimulative economic policies. Moreover, the inflationary pressures stemming from the sharp increase in the price of oil are now in the past, as oil price *declines* have replaced increases. Under these circumstances, no worldwide economic boom is in prospect nor is a quick return to the inflationary era of the seventies. These developments suggest that we have finally come to the end of the great bear market in interest rates.

The situation, however, is by no means that clear-cut. On statistical grounds alone, there is room for doubt. Since the secular peak was reached in long-term rates in October 1981, no full cyclical swing in interest rates has yet been recorded. Interest rates have fallen since October 1981, but they have not yet risen cyclically, so that the 1981 highs are still untested. A rise through the secular high would reaffirm the secular trend, while a failure to do so, a cyclical peak that falls short of the 1981 highs, would imply that the great bear market has run out of steam.

A fundamental question arises regarding the extent to which the many changes that have been taking place in financial behavior—particularly financial innovations, deregulation, and the trend toward short-term or floating-rate financing—will have a lasting influence on interest rates.

In addition, the continued rapid growth of debt in the United States contributes toward eventual higher, not lower, rates. The

131

absence of a well-balanced monetary-fiscal policy is a major element in that picture. Continued large federal budget deficits will force the Federal Reserve to rely on a rise in rates to curb the next period of economic excess, running the risk of much higher rates than would be required if the budget deficit were under control.

Recognizing these uncertainties, I have nevertheless come to some tentative conclusions about the secular trend of interest rates. First, that the secular rate rise in the *money market* has probably been arrested. The increasing volume of short-term and floating-rate financing will make the private sector quickly vulnerable to the cost of a higher debt burden when interest rates rise the next time around. The increase in debt burden will preempt a significant portion of household and corporate income, curbing more quickly than heretofore the activities of these two sectors.

On the other hand, two credit market developments force me to be somewhat uncertain about the secular trend of *long-term* rates. One is the near-term performance of institutional investors, who in the restructured markets of recent decades generally will not commit funds long when short rates are rising. The other development is the continued large supply of intermediate and long-term Governments that is likely to be forthcoming during the next period of monetary restraint. There is a fair chance that long yields will stay below their secular peaks, but the certainty of such an event would be greatly enhanced with a sharp slowing of U.S. Government bond issuance and with the emergence of intermediate and longer-term investment decisions by portfolio managers.

CYCLICAL TRENDS

I will confine my analysis of cyclical swings in interest rates to those cyclical movements that have taken place during the great secular bear market that has dominated the years following the end of World War II. Since 1949/50, the long relentless rise in yields has encompassed six cyclical bear markets and six cyclical bull markets.

Chart 12 gives a vivid picture of the postwar secular rise and cyclical swings of interest rates. The six bear markets (rising rates) are from 1949/50 to 1953, from 1954 to 1957, from 1958 to 1959/60, from 1963 to 1970, from 1971/72 to 1974, and from 1977 to 1981. The six bull markets (falling rates) are 1953 to 1954, 1957 to 1958, 1959/60 to 1963, 1970 to 1971/72, 1974 to 1977, and since 1981.

The magnitudes of the cyclical upswings in interest rates have consistently been much larger than the downswings. In other words, successive peaks have exceeded prior peaks, while successive troughs have not gone as low as prior troughs. The

Chart 12. Prime Long Corporate Bonds, 1946–85

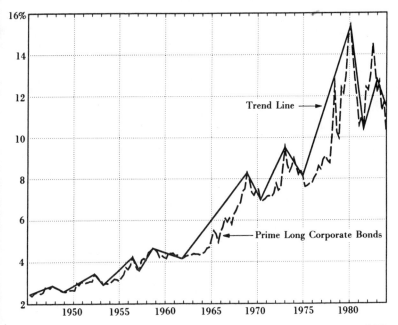

Table 8. Duration of Bear Market Cycles of Selected Long-Term and Short-Term Interest Rates (in Months)

	Cycles Beginning							
	1949–50	1954	1958	1961–63	1971–72	1977–81	1983[a]	Avg.[b]
Long-term								
Governments	41	36	24	107	33	57	9	50
New Aa Utilities	43	41	20	88	43	57	9	49
30-year Prime Municipals	28	37	20	91	45	57	9	46
Average Long-term	37	38	21	95	40	57	9	48
Intermediate (7 to 10 Year)								
Governments	41	41	20	108	41	56	9	51
Short-term (3-month)								
Treasury Bills	45	40	18	112	41	57	9	52
Commercial Paper/CD	43	38	20	104	32	60	9	50
Average Short-term	44	39	19	108	37	59	9	51

[a]Incomplete cycle.
[b]Excludes 1983.

dominance of the underlying secular bear market trend is strikingly evident from the difference between the long duration of cyclical increases in rates compared to the relatively short periods of downturns. The cyclical increases in rates have lasted 48 months on average as compared with declines averaging only 15 months. There has been very little difference between the duration of cyclical movements in short rates and long rates (see Tables 8 and 9).

Within the bond markets, there have been no individual star performers during the postwar years, although a slight edge must be given to long Governments during cyclical rises in interest rates. During those periods, yields on Governments frequently rose by less than yields on corporates and municipals.

One reason for this is the legal 4¼ percent coupon ceiling that for many years prevented the Treasury from issuing a large volume of new long bonds. This inhibition on new supply helped limit yield increases on Governments relative to corporates and municipals. In addition, another reason surfaced during the worst cyclical fall in bond prices, the years from 1977 to 1981: a strong preference for quality combined with the enhanced liquidity provided by a rapidly growing market for Government futures kept Government rates from rising as much as other bond yields.

EXTREMES IN QUALITY YIELD SPREADS

Another repetitive pattern in interest rates is the difference in interest-rate movements between issuers of varying credit quality. To illustrate, Table 10 shows three sectors: the money market (3-month negotiable CDs versus Treasury bills), the municipal bond market (A-rated versus AAA-rated general obligations), and the corporate bond market (BBB versus AA utilities).

In the money market, the maximum yield spreads generally occur shortly after a cyclical peak in economic activity. In the

Table 9. Duration of Bull Market Cycles of Selected Long-Term and Short-Term Interest Rates (in Months)

	Cycles Beginning						
	1953	*1957*	*1959–60*	*1970*	*1974*	*1981*	*Avg.*
Long-term							
Governments	14	5	17	18	27	19	17
New Aa Utilities	9	6	40	7	27	19	18
30-year Prime Municipals	4	4	37	19	15	20	17
Average Long-term	9	5	31	15	23	19	27
Intermediate (7 to 10 Year)							
Governments	10	7	15	14	27	19	15
Short-term (3-month)							
Treasury Bills	14	8	8	15	27	29	17
Commercial Paper	13	8	16	24	27	29	20
Average Short-term	14	8	12	25	27	29	19

Table 10. Extreme Yield Spreads: 3-month CDs versus Treasury Bills (in Basis Points)

Maximum	4/60	12/69	11/73	1/80	7/81
	75	210	482	395	290
Minimum	2/61	11/70	3/75	7/80	11/82
	0	32	14	50	18

Extreme Municipal Bond Quality Yield Spreads: A versus AAA-rated General Obligations (in Basis Points)

Maximum	4/60	12/69	11/73	1/80	7/81
	50	115	90	75	125
Minimum	2/61	11/70	3/75	7/80	11/82
	15	20	20	50	50

Extreme Corporate Bond Quality Yield Spreads: BBB versus AA Utilities (in Basis Points)

Maximum	12/69	11/73	1/80	7/81
		365	200	187
Minimum	11/70	3/75	7/80	11/82
	35	45	137	50

early sixties, when the negotiable CD market was just starting, extreme spreads were moderate as compared with maximum spreads of 300 to 500 basis points reached in the seventies and later.

These wide spreads reflected brief moments in which there was not only a general preference for liquidity but also, occasionally, specific concerns related to the financial difficulties of a few banking institutions. In contrast, *minimum* CD-Treasury bill spreads take place most of the time when a business recovery has been underway for about three or four months.

Extremes in quality spreads in the corporate and municipal bond markets are not as great as in the money market. Municipal spreads (A versus AAA-rated general obligations) widened to a new cyclical peak of 182 basis points in early 1982 and then collapsed to a cyclical low of 50 basis points later in the year.

In the corporate bond market, yield spreads between AA and BBB-rated utilities hit a cyclical maximum of 365 basis points in 1974 when the financial problems of Consolidated Edison caused investor apprehension. Minimum cyclical spreads of 35 to 50 basis points occur when interest rates recede.

INTEREST RATES AND ECONOMIC ACTIVITY

While rising interest rates are generally identified with periods of economic expansion and declining rates with business contractions, these posited relationships are oversimplifications. Tables 11 and 12 compare the timing of peaks and troughs in yields relative to peaks and troughs in economic activity.

Table 11 shows that the *peak* in yields came just before the 1953 peak in business conditions; came after the crest in business in 1957; substantially preceded the end of the boom in 1960; came well after the end of the business expansions that terminated in 1969, 1973, and the truncated 1980 cycle; and short rates preceded while long rates lagged the July 1981 economic peak. Particularly in the long bond market, interest rates have tended to top out *after* business recessions have begun.

With respect to cyclical *troughs,* Table 12 shows that in the early cycles after World War II yields in most sectors reached their lows just before the end of the recession (see 1954 and 1958). Since then, however, the opposite has generally been the case: interest rates have typically continued to fall well past the

Table 11. Number of Months by Which the Cyclical Peak in Interest Rates Preceded (+) or (Lagged (−) the Peak in Economic Activity

| | Peak in Economic Activity | | | | | | |
	7/53	8/57	4/60	11/69	11/73	1/80	7/81
Short-term							
Treasury Bills	+3	−2	+5	−1	−9	−3	+2
Commercial Paper	+1	−1	+3	−2	−9	−3	+2
Long-term							
U.S. Government Bonds	+1	0	+3	−7	−9	−1	−2
Corporate Bonds	+1	0	+6	−8	−11	−3	−2
Municipal Bonds	+1	−1	+8	−8	−8	−3	−2

Table 12. Number of Months by Which the Cyclical Trough in Interest Rates Preceded (+) or Lagged (−) the Trough in Economic Activity

| | Trough in Economic Activity | | | | | | |
	5/54	4/58	2/61	11/70	3/75[a]	7/80	11/82
Short-term							
Treasury Bills	−1	−2	+6	−15	−21	+1	−6
Commercial Paper	−2	−1	−3	−14	−21	+1	−6
Long-term							
U.S. Government Bonds	−3	+3	−4	−12	−21	+1	−6
Corporate Bonds	+2	+2	−24	−2	−21	+1	−6
Municipal Bonds	−3	+3	−21	−14	−21	+2	−6

[a]May be an incomplete cycle.

onset of economic revival. In some instances (1961 and 1975), rates continued down for close to two years after business turned up.

CONVENTIONAL WISDOMS

This evidence should caution those who try to gauge the timing of interest-rate directions merely by relating them to changes in economic activity. Even so, and no matter what the difficulties, there is generally no lack of portfolio managers anxious to plunge in and anticipate the next cyclical change in interest rates. What is the explanation for the ever-present feverish desire to call the turn on the next major cyclical movement in the bond market?

In our time, the continuous measurement of portfolio performance has driven portfolio managers to plunge ahead with long commitments, fearing that otherwise a rally might be unused; thus missing a rally, they would fall behind in the competitive struggle to attract new funds into the portfolio.

In addition, a series of conventional wisdoms encourage the commitment of funds prematurely. Some are political and others are economic or financial. Here are samplings of political assessments that are supposed to suggest, for instance, an imminent decline in interest rates:

1. The federal government will not tolerate a rise in interest rates, because it threatens the business recovery.
2. With an election year ahead, interest rates will soon begin to decline.
3. The new president (or secretary of the treasury or chairman of the Federal Reserve) will fight inflation without permitting rates to rise.

These political samplings require no detailed commentary: they do not stand the test of history. They are based on subjective rather than objective appraisals of the forces over which politicians can exercise control in the near term.

Conventional *financial* wisdoms are far more dangerous because they at first appear to have a sound rationale. One is the belief that a slackening in prospective credit demands equates with declining interest rates. The facts refute this; credit demands usually begin to moderate *prior* to the peak in interest rates.

Another false observation holds that a reduction in U.S. Government financing will be a major factor in pulling interest rates down. This supposition also appears persuasive until examined carefully. Interest rates in 1979, for example, rose sharply even though the market financing requirements of the Treasury were declining substantially. In contrast, Treasury needs soared from 1974 to 1975, but interest rates fell. In general, rates depend less on the Treasury's needs than on the composition of other credit demands, the magnitude of real resource utilization, expected inflation, and monetary policy, among other things. As in most areas of economics and finance, simple rule-of-thumb formulas rarely provide satisfactory answers consistently.

CHAPTER 12

The Many Faces of the Yield Curve

Changes in financial behavior have had a significant impact on the term structure of interest rates and its graphic representation, the yield curve. The behavior of the yield curve is not the same as it was a generation or two ago. As a result, undue dependence on the yield curve as a harbinger of changes in interest-rate directions can be dangerous and costly.

Nevertheless, yield curves can still provide a sweeping picture of credit market conditions at a glance and at times a close examination may offer arbitraging and swapping opportunities. Because of the new behavior and structure of financial markets, riding the yield curve correctly can bestow quick riches; riding the curve wrongly, however, invites investment decapitation.

THEORIES

For many years, there have been a number of theories regarding the term structure of interest rates. One of the oldest, and still one of the most popular, is the "expectations theory." This theory holds that the long-term rate is an average of the current short-term rate and short rates that are expected to prevail in the future. The relationship between the yield on a long-term security and the yield on a short-term security depends on expected future short-term rates.

If expected future short rates are above the current short rate, then the current long rate will be above the current short rate and the yield curve will be upward-sloping. But if expected future short rates are below the current short-term rate, then the current long rate will be below the current short rate and the yield curve will be downward-sloping.

The implication of an upward-sloping yield curve is that market participants expect interest rates to rise. A downward-sloping yield curve reflects expectations that rates will fall, while a flat curve suggests they will remain unchanged.

Typically, of course, yield curves that slope sharply downward—with short rates much higher than long rates—are eventually followed by movements to flat and then to upward-sloping yield curves. In the transition, short rates decline more than longs. Conversely, sharply upward-sloping yield curves eventually become flat and then downward-sloping, with short rates increasing more than long rates.

An alternative theory emphasizes market segmentation more than expectations; it implies that short and long securities are not perfect substitutes for each other in investor portfolios, so that rates are heavily influenced by the preferences and rigidities of institutional participants in the market. Lenders and borrowers are believed to have such strong maturity preferences that they will not depart from their habitual investment practices to take advantage of yield differentials. Accordingly, there are a number

Chart 13. U.S Government Yield Curves

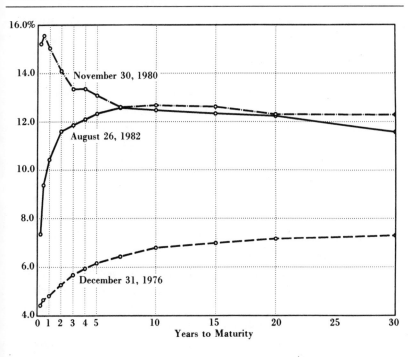

of different maturity sectors in the market where rates are determined by compartmentalized supply-and-demand factors.

The aforementioned view that expectations regarding future short-term rates determine the shape of the yield curve is not the only "expectations" theory of term structure. Another view is that the key lies in expected future *long-term* interest rates. This starts with the observation that upward-sloping yield curves are typical of recessions, while downward-sloping ones are characteristic of boom periods. Why is this so?

The long-term rate expectations analysis runs in terms of standard Keynesian liquidity preference interest theory. When long-term rates *fall too low,* investors start expecting that they are likely to rise—that is, that long-term bond prices will plum-

143

met. On the other hand, when long-term rates *rise too high*, investors start expecting that they will fall—that is, that long-term bond prices will skyrocket. When investors behave rationally to avoid capital losses or obtain capital gains on long-term securities (selling them when they think the price will fall and buying them when they think the price will rise), the result is the yield curves typical of various phases of the business cycle.

For example, once long-term yields have fallen during a recession to the point where they are not expected to fall further, investors tend to liquidate their long bonds, fearing capital losses. They put the proceeds into Treasury bills or other short-term money market instruments, where prices are not as responsive to interest-rate changes. The move out of long bonds into short bills tends to check the fall in bond yields while simultaneously driving bill rates lower, producing an upward-sloping yield curve.

Similarly, once long rates have risen to the point where they are not expected to rise further, investors tend to sell bills and buy bonds, hoping for capital gains. This checks the rise in bond yields while driving bill rates higher, producing a downward-sloping yield curve.

Borrower behavior is postulated to reinforce these yield-curve effects. Borrowers tend to borrow long rather than short when long rates are cyclically low, and short rather than long when long rates are cyclically high.

What insights do these theories hold for portfolio managers? To be sure, upward or downward extremes in the slopes of yield curves can help gauge market direction but, as discussed below, this information can be very costly if not treated with prudence. The vast changes that have occurred in credit markets in recent decades are leaving their marks on the behavior of the yield curve, so that historical experience is no longer an adequate guide. The increased popularity of monetarism, deregulation, the rapid growth of debt, and other developments explored in detail elsewhere in this book have all affected the yield curve in one way or another. Deregulation and the cross-fertilization of markets, for example, have disrupted maturity preferences and investment habits of long standing and significantly weakened market segmentation.

As a result, the following aspects of the yield curve deserve special mention:

1. There is more than one single yield curve for analytical purposes. Each has distinctive characteristics.
2. Yield curves have become highly volatile.
3. Yield curves no longer fluctuate within well-defined historical limits.
4. Cyclical extremes in interest rates typically do not coincide with cyclical extremes in yield curves.
5. The correlation between economic activity and yield curves is not high. The relationship, in fact, varies considerably.

FOUR MAJOR YIELD CURVES

Among the many yield curves in the various markets for fixed-income obligations, four are most frequently used by financial analysts:

1. yield differentials between 1-year and 3-month Treasury bills
2. yield differentials between 30-year and 3-month seasoned U.S. Governments
3. yield differentials between 30-year new AA utilities and 3-month commercial paper
4. yield differentials between 30-year and 1-year prime municipal general obligations

All four yield curves are shown in Chart 14 from 1960 through 1984.

Chart 14. Long- versus Short-Yield Differentials in Four Sectors of the Debt Markets, 1960–85 (Monthly Data in Basis Points)

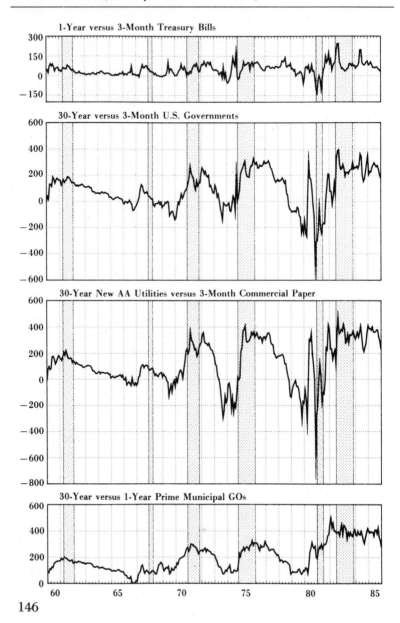

1-Year versus 3-Month Treasury Bills

30-Year versus 3-Month U.S. Governments

30-Year New AA Utilities versus 3-Month Commercial Paper

30-Year versus 1-Year Prime Municipal GOs

Among the four, Treasury bill yield differentials show the most consistent pattern, fluctuating most of the time between zero and a positive 100 basis points. The municipal yield curve, uniquely, is always positively sloped (long rates higher than short), but the extent depends on the phase of the business and monetary policy cycles.

In contrast, the other two—Governments and corporates— are virtually parallel in their movements. Periodically, both have turned either negative or positive.

As Chart 14 indicates, yield curves in general have become much more volatile than they were in the past. It is no accident that the increased volatility dates from the end of 1979 and the beginning of 1980, which is also when the Federal Reserve adopted, at least for a few years, a hard-line monetarist position.

Given the basic principle that one can control either the price or the quantity but not both, interest rates under monetarism fluctuated without restraint as the by-product of a predetermined rate of money supply growth. The Fed chose to control the quantity of money and let interest rates find their own level. The results in terms of rate volatility are clearly visible in Chart 14.

For many years, the traditional wisdom was that the optimum time to buy long-term securities is when the yield curve slopes downward most sharply—often called the point of maximum inversion in the yield curve. That is, it was believed that the best time to make long-term commitments is when short rates are at their maximum differential *above* long rates. Such a condition was considered a signal that shortly the yield curve would return to "normal" (that is, would first flatten out and then once more become upward-sloping).

In the process of the yield curve returning to "normal," it was expected that both short rates *and* long rates would fall, with short rates falling further than long rates to restore an upward slope. It was the expected decline in long rates that was the crux

147

of the matter, however, since even modest declines in long-term yields can produce substantial capital gains.

This conventional wisdom is no longer creditable. The reason is that in recent decades the yield curve, after reaching the point of maximum inversion, has typically flattened *not* by short rates falling further than longs, but rather by long rates *rising* while shorter rates fell.

In other words, maximum inversion in the yield curve presents not a golden opportunity but just the opposite: an immediate period of danger as far as investing in long-term bonds is concerned. For example, following the maximum yield inversion in December 1980, long Governments and corporate bond yields rose by nearly another 200 to 300 basis points. This painful experience in long bond performance following the benchmark extreme yield curve inversions in Governments lasted 5 months in 1969/70, 12 months in 1973/74, and 9 months in 1980/81. The two exceptions were in 1960 and in April 1980, when the maximum yield inversions nearly coincided with peaks in long-term interest rates.

THE OPTIMUM LONG OPPORTUNITY

If the risk in investing in the long market is still great immediately following the point of maximum inversion, when does the long market offer the best opportunity? To answer this question, it is necessary to examine the swings in the U.S. Government securities yield curve during the past quarter century (see Table 13).

These swings are:

1. from extreme negative (short rates above long) to flat
2. from flat to extreme positive (long rates above short)
3. from extreme positive to flat
4. from flat to extreme negative

Table 13. Net Short- and Long-Yield Changes during Cyclical Swings in the Yield Curve: Government and Corporates (in Basis Points)

	1959–70		1970–73		1973–80		1980		1980–84	
	Short	Long	Short	Long	Short	Long	Short	Long	Short	Long
Governments[a]										
Extreme Negative to Flat	−17	20	−113	45	56	138	−583	−191	−380	121
Flat to Extreme Positive	−224	−34	−366	−113	−459	−69	−441	−119	−696	−210
Extreme Positive to Flat	236	40	362	97	371	60	571	220	336*	−7*
Flat to Extreme Negative	365	232	174	24	810	396	609	145		
Corporates[b]										
Extreme Negative to Flat	13	15	−26	115	−173	120	−519	−100	−361	263
Flat to Extreme Positive	−258	−30	−458	−100	−369	−5	−374	25	−880	−325
Extreme Positive to Flat	494	260	326	−35	400	30	524	162	266*	−87*
Flat to Extreme Negative	158	40	358	55	835	383	675	50		

[a]U.S. Governments: 3-month bill (bond yield equivalent) and 30-year bonds.
[b]Corporates: 3-month commercial paper (bond yield equivalent) and Salomon Brothers, Inc., estimate of new long AA utility bonds.
*Incomplete. Yield change to least positive yield curve (Sept. 1984) since 1982.

The results are as follows:

1. When the yield curve for government securities swung from extreme negative to flat, long yields actually increased with one exception—the 1980 cycle. In one of these cycles, there was a greater rise in long yields than in short rates. In all other instances, however, short rates fell while long yields rose.

2. When the yield curve moved from flat to extreme positive, with long yields going above short, in all cycles long yields fell in conjunction with a more sizable drop in short rates.

3. The swing from extreme positive to flat can be quite dangerous in the long bond sector. In the four complete cycles shown in Table 13, yield increases averaged 104 basis points for long-term issues, ranging from 40 to 220 basis points.

4. The most dangerous period of all for investors in long bonds, however, occurs when the yield curve moves from flat to extremely negative, with short rates shooting up above long. As the table indicates, long rates increased by 199 basis points on average during such periods, ranging from 24 to 396 basis points.

Similar conclusions can be drawn from the data shown for corporates in Table 13. The same lesson is demonstrated again and again: in this turbulent day and age, neither enlightenment nor profits can be gained by reliance on the unexamined wisdom of the past.

PROSPECTS

While the yield curve has become quite volatile and inversions common, the slope of the curve may again be undergoing change. For several reasons, yield inversions may occur very late in a business expansion or may not occur at all. Disintermediation is no longer likely to take place during cyclical increases in interest rates because Regulation Q is no longer important. Deposit-type institutions can now pay market rates and hold on to their depositors.

There is also the desire of borrowers to finance short and the strong preference by lenders for such short-maturity interest-rate-linked obligations as floating-rate notes and variable-rate mortgages. In addition, the rapidly expanding volume of marketable obligations, combined with the related short-term preference horizons of investors, will discourage investors from committing funds long when there is no prospect of a meaningful drop in short rates.

There are at least two circumstances in which the yield curve might be inverted. One would require the U.S. Treasury to sharply curtail its bond issues. The other would require the Federal Reserve to tighten credit sharply several times over a short time span. Short rates would then take quantum jumps; for example, 200 or 300 basis points in a matter of a few weeks. This would render impossible the arbitraging of the yield curve by market participants, and short rates would spike above long rates. Such movements would be reinforced if the Fed reverted to a close adherence to monetarism.

CHAPTER 13

Changing Techniques in Forecasting Interest Rates

Not many years ago, Salomon Brothers' interest-rate forecasts were based in large measure on an analysis of domestic credit flows, a technique that was widely known as the supply-and-demand-for-credit method of interest-rate forecasting, also sometimes called the flow-of-funds analytical method.

This is no longer the case. In fact, it would now be almost as accurate to say that a judgment about the trend of interest rates based on *other* considerations determines the configuration of Salomon Brothers' credit flow projections. To understand this 180-degree turnabout, one must appreciate the extent to which the deregulation of financial markets has altered the relationship between credit flows and the cost of funds.

ANTICIPATION AND REALIZATION

The distinction between *anticipation* and *realization* is crucial to the relationship between credit flows and the cost of funds. Anticipation, of course, refers to what might reasonably be expected to occur *before* it happens, while realization refers, *after the fact,* to what actually took place. For example, if within the context of rising employment and a vigorous economy, the prevailing level of mortgage rates suggests a flood of loan applications to highly liquid lending institutions, one would anticipate mortgage lending to rise substantially during the coming months. However, whether mortgage lending will actually in fact rise as much as expected depends on a number of other related factors.

If the U.S. Treasury, for instance, planned an increase in bill financing—even if that increase were widely expected and generally reflected in the current level of bill yields—actually realized mortgage formation might fall short of anticipations. Why? Because bill rates might rise, siphoning funds from the mortgage market, with the consequence that mortgage rates also rise, reducing the amount of mortgages demanded.

Fundamental to a possible disparity between what is anticipated and what is realized is the extent to which current market prices reflect future developments. Interest rates are just another price—the price of borrowing money. Current prices in just about any market represent some consensus about probable future prices. But it would be naive to believe that this consensus reflects *all* relevant probable future developments, to say nothing of wholly unpredictable events and their impact.

Credit flow analysis can no more address these erratic events than can individual market participants; it can, however, more systematically catch all of the reasonably predictable developments, especially those that are a reasoned response to the current level of interest rates.

In the mortgage example above, the Treasury bill yield may

already reflect as much information about Treasury financing as is available to the credit flow analyst. But it is not likely to fully reflect such factors as a future diminished interest in Treasury securities on the part of mortgage lending institutions when these institutions are currently buying at a rapid pace. The bill market might be marked by higher rates, and consequently by a reduced incentive, at least short term, for savers to roll over savings accounts at lending institutions. Mortgage lending might therefore turn out to be less than anticipated.

This simple distinction between anticipation and realization is at the heart of all credit flow supply-and-demand analyses. Specific methods of applying the distinction might differ. One strategy, used by Salomon Brothers in the past, would be to independently calculate all the anticipatory elements *supplying* credit at current interest rates and all the anticipatory elements *demanding* credit at current rates, and then to compare the two. If the demand for credit at current rates exceeds the supply, the implication is that interest rates will rise; whereas if the supply for credit at current rates exceeds the demand, rates will be forecast to fall.

The second phase of the analysis is to attempt the same kind of rationing that the market applies—changing the level of rates, up or down, as indicated by the relationship between demand and supply, and then comparing amounts supplied and demanded once again. Based on the typical supply-and-demand curves taught in elementary economics courses, higher interest rates imply smaller amounts of credit demanded and larger amounts supplied, while lower rates produce larger amounts demanded and smaller amounts supplied.

That is, if the demand for funds exceeds the supply, interest rates will have to rise to eliminate the weaker, interest-sensitive, would-be borrowers and to lure interest-sensitive suppliers (lenders) to the market. On the other hand, if the supply of funds is greater than the demand for them, some investors will probably outbid others for the available securities, pushing securities prices up and interest rates down, thereby attracting additional borrowing.

This is obviously an iterative device that constantly modifies one's premises at the start of each iteration—not only for interest rates but also for fundamental marginal propensities and the pace of economic and financial activity. The process of successive approximations continues until the amount of credit supplied and the amount demanded are equal. Once the amounts supplied and demanded are equal, there is no longer pressure forcing interest rates up or down (that is, the market is in equilibrium).

A sophisticated refinement known as "residual analysis" involves finding the particularly interest-sensitive investment funds in total supply. For years, this was identified with foreign investment and direct (i.e., nonintermediated) investment by the household sector. But for a variety of reasons, mentioned below, this process is no longer wholly reliable.

One unfortunate aspect of the credit flow approach to interest-rate developments has always been that the conclusions are not necessarily reflected in the results. The conclusions cannot be approached except through the difficult process of working an anticipatory imbalance through to a realized balance, thereby finding the likely changes in interest rates needed to equilibrate the credit markets.

These methods worked well in the regulated financial marketplace of the sixties and seventies. They not only correctly predicted the "credit crunch" that produced century-high long-term interest rates in 1966, but also correctly predicted that the nearly unanimous optimistic economic forecasts of that era would prove to be erroneous.

In the late sixties, the sum of all the anticipated credit demands needed to finance expected record housing activity and business capital expenditures, on top of a huge budgeted in-

155

crease in spending for the war in Vietnam, was obviously far in excess of anticipated savings and monetary expansion. The predicted interest-rate increases drove funds away from deposit-type institutions that were hampered by restrictions on their ability to compete for savings—as Regulation Q produced financial disintermediation—and the analysis correctly forecast eventual disappointment for many would-be borrowers.

THE EFFECTS OF DEREGULATION

A largely unforeseen consequence of the series of credit crises in the sixties and seventies was a successful campaign by the afflicted financial institutions for relief from regulatory crunch and loss. Ironically, deregulation has so altered the process of monetary restraint that credit flow analysis has become far more difficult to interpret. The straightforward method of translating changes in interest rates imposed by Federal Reserve policy into changes in the pattern of credit flows no longer exists.

Thrift institutions, for example, can now maintain their level of savings flows by matching changes in competing market interest rates, thereby thwarting disintermediation. And when narrowing maturity yield curves reduce their profit margins dangerously, thrifts no longer need slow the pace of mortgage lending. They merely act as mortgage bankers rather than investors and package new loans in mortgage pools for sale to contractual savings institutions such as insurance companies and pension funds.

Ultimately, of course, this drives rates up to the point where the effective demand for loans by home buyers diminishes. However, even this point can be deferred for some time through the use of variable-rate loans.

What is left for the credit flow analyst? Where is the telltale in the accounts or analysis that can substitute for the process of disintermediation?

Over the past several years, we at Salomon Brothers have redirected our attention to a more fundamental level of the accounts: we now focus on anticipated changes in the sum of (1) the federal deficit, (2) household net financial saving, and (3) the deficit for nonfinancial corporations.

In other words, we try to determine if an overall balance or imbalance exists at the level of the aggregate surplus or deficit of the domestic nonfinancial sectors. Unfortunately, at least in the short run and probably longer, policy-induced changes in the Federal funds rate can and probably will override any anticipated domestic impulses that would otherwise have operated in the other direction.

In regulated markets, anticipated imbalances tended to self-correct in a relatively short time period. The 1966 credit crunch, for example, lasted barely four months. The imbalances could be trusted to drive up interest rates, limited by the consequent period of disintermediation. Interest-sensitive types of economic activity collapsed, and all concerned revised their plans in light of the changed economic circumstances.

Now, however, rising interest rates no longer produce large-scale outflows of funds from thrifts and similar deposit-type institutions. Deregulation has enabled these institutions to cope rather easily with rising rates—or at least to ride the tide much longer than before.

Higher rates now pull in funds from outside the system, from abroad. If left to purely domestic factors, the process would continue to push up rates until a prohibitive cost of money forced economic activity to stall. That stall-out rate level, however, is far less predictable and far less imminent in the absence of disintermediation.

There are no longer compelling rational reasons to radically reformulate borrowing or lending plans merely because the Federal Reserve happens to increase the Federal funds rate by 50 or even 100 basis points. The interest-rate structure that any given set of anticipated domestic credit flows is likely to produce is irrelevant. The realized flows will be shaped by a level of rates determined by the Fed.

INTERNATIONAL CREDIT FLOWS

That would indeed be the situation were it not for the fact that we now have a new marginally sensitive participant in the markets to replace households—and thus a new form of residual analysis. The extent of foreign participation necessary to clear the accounts is given by the anticipated domestic imbalance. The price at which these foreign funds become available is determined by a number of factors: the pace of economic activity abroad, the strength of other currencies relative to the U.S. dollar, and the actions of foreign central banks, to name but three.

The Federal Reserve, therefore, has to adjust its policy to create this available supply, often in competition with foreign central banks. The latter may wish to hold savings at home rather than see them migrate to the United States, or may wish to maintain the strength of their own currencies relative to the U.S. dollar. Or their willingness to compete for these savings might be limited if their economies are weak.

The extension of the analysis to international credit flows is not new. What *is* new is its paramount analytic importance.

OTHER BENEFITS FROM CREDIT FLOW ANALYSIS

While great care is needed in using flow of funds analysis to predict interest rates, funds analysis is nevertheless extremely helpful in other respects. It provides perspective and, like double-entry bookkeeping, contains built-in features that help prevent errors in logic.

Table 14, for example, shows flows of funds annually for the period 1966 through 1984. In the final analysis, as the table indicates for each year, the amount of funds supplied must equal the amount demanded because it is impossible to lend money unless someone borrows it. In a market economy, the function of prices is to allocate scarce resources; in financial markets, this means that the function of interest rates is to allocate the funds supplied by lenders among those want to borrow.

The perspective provided by credit flow analysis prevents one from adopting some popular but incorrect conventional wisdoms. Here are two illustrations. First, increases in overall effective demands for credit do not necessarily mean that interest rates will rise. Typically, in the early stages of economic recovery net credit flows rise sharply but interest rates *decline.* In contrast, increases in overall credit demands when the economy is near what used to be called "full employment" (defined as consistent with 6 percent unemployment), pushes interest rates up. Numerous instances of this varying pattern can be seen in Chart 15.

The second illustration involves the corporate sector. The volume of new corporate bond financing is not the trigger that tends to tighten credit market conditions. Usually what tightens the credit markets is a rapid increase in *total* external corporate financing, which includes short- and long-term borrowings of all sorts. Chart 16 shows that the bank prime loan rate tends to rise when corporate external financing increases, and it tends to fall when these demands for credit abate. Corporate treasurers often try to finance through bonds when interest rates are declining and rely on short-term funds when credit conditions are tight and interest rates rising.

Supply and demand for credit analysis also clearly identifies the competitive strength of various groups of credit demanders. The last few decades have shown that despite the presumed

Table 14. Net Changes in the Supply and Demand for Credit
(Dollars in Billions)

	1966	1967	1968	1969	1970	1971	1972	1973
Net Demand								
Mortgages	23.6	23.6	29.6	30.7	29.3	50.6	75.6	80.7
Corporate and Foreign Bonds	11.2	16.6	14.4	13.8	24.4	24.7	20.3	14.6
Long-term Private	34.8	40.2	44.0	44.5	53.7	75.2	95.9	95.2
Short-term Business	14.0	10.6	18.0	29.3	9.4	10.9	27.7	57.2
Short-term Household	13.4	8.2	19.8	26.6	12.9	18.2	28.3	44.4
Short-term Private	27.4	18.8	37.8	55.8	22.3	29.1	56.0	101.6
U.S. Government Debt	9.2	13.2	17.4	6.2	21.7	30.9	23.6	28.3
State and Local Government Debt	5.6	7.8	9.5	9.9	11.2	17.4	14.7	14.7
Total Government Debt	14.8	21.0	26.9	16.1	32.9	48.3	38.3	43.0
Total Net Demand	77.1	79.9	108.7	116.4	108.9	152.6	190.1	239.8
Net Supply								
Households	15.7	6.2	15.8	38.3	3.7	−4.3	9.8	36.7
Corporate Business	−0.9	−1.3	2.7	−1.1	2.1	6.5	2.8	−1.4
State and Local	2.3	0.3	2.4	4.7	−1.9	−0.2	6.9	5.6
Foreign	−1.6	2.0	0.3	−0.5	10.5	26.4	8.4	0.6
U.S. Government	5.1	4.7	5.2	3.1	2.8	2.8	1.8	3.9
Agencies, Mortgage Pools, Fed	9.0	5.4	7.4	13.5	15.3	14.7	9.1	28.4
Banking	17.6	36.1	38.8	19.0	35.7	50.4	70.3	84.7
Thrifts	9.3	14.1	15.7	14.6	17.0	37.0	45.1	34.3
Insurance	16.1	13.0	13.7	13.2	17.0	13.6	21.5	28.2
Other Nonbank Finance	4.6	−0.7	6.5	11.5	6.8	5.6	14.3	18.9
Total Net Supply	77.1	79.9	108.7	116.4	108.9	152.6	190.1	239.8

1974	1975	1976	1977	1978	1979	1980	1981	1982	1983	1984
64.5	57.9	85.4	126.2	152.1	166.1	129.3	108.4	86.2	175.6	213.9
24.9	36.7	41.2	38.0	32.8	29.0	29.3	30.7	35.0	28.4	64.8
89.4	94.5	126.6	164.3	184.9	195.1	158.6	139.2	121.2	204.0	287.7
59.1	−13.4	14.5	44.9	85.2	93.2	68.3	113.2	54.8	51.9	118.0
32.4	19.4	43.2	67.7	90.7	87.9	44.8	79.0	39.8	75.3	151.4
91.5	6.0	57.8	112.6	175.9	181.1	113.1	192.2	94.6	127.2	269.4
31.9	94.9	83.8	79.9	90.5	84.8	122.9	133.0	225.9	254.4	273.8
16.5	16.1	15.7	21.9	28.4	30.3	30.3	23.4	48.6	57.3	65.8
48.4	111.0	99.4	101.8	118.8	115.1	153.1	156.4	274.5	311.8	339.5
229.3	211.6	283.8	378.7	479.6	491.3	424.9	487.8	490.2	643.0	887.6
36.8	25.3	22.9	29.4	47.5	73.0	30.8	53.9	48.6	74.7	123.9
7.6	12.3	8.0	−5.3	3.7	5.2	−2.2	11.5	12.8	20.4	22.2
0.1	1.9	7.7	12.4	13.2	21.6	17.9	7.4	27.2	47.7	46.1
11.2	6.1	15.2	39.6	33.3	−4.5	23.3	16.2	22.8	27.1	43.4
9.4	13.4	7.9	10.0	17.1	19.0	23.7	24.0	15.9	9.7	17.2
30.3	20.1	26.7	29.7	47.2	60.7	50.1	57.4	75.3	80.7	81.7
67.0	29.5	59.8	87.8	128.5	123.1	100.6	102.3	107.2	136.1	181.9
25.3	50.9	68.4	78.5	72.2	56.5	54.5	27.4	31.4	140.5	143.0
35.8	52.0	55.7	73.1	89.3	85.6	94.5	97.6	107.4	94.2	123.1
5.7	0.0	11.4	23.6	27.6	51.2	31.7	89.9	41.5	11.9	105.1
229.3	211.6	283.8	378.7	479.6	491.3	424.9	487.8	490.2	643.0	887.6

Chart 15. Incremental Change in Net Demand for Credit (Dollars in Billions) versus Long U.S. Government Bond Yields, 1966–85

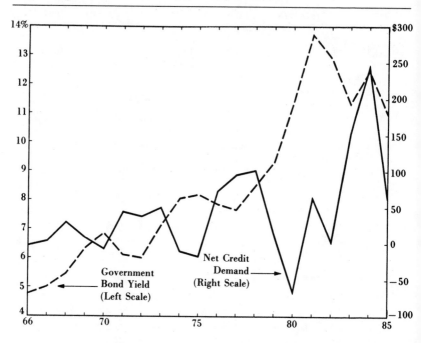

benefits of deregulation and financial innovation, some credit demanders cannot survive the competitive struggle when credit availability shrinks.

Borrowing for home mortgages is the prime example in this connection. Although new federal credit agencies have been established to cushion the impact of tight money on housing, and new and highly flexible as well as marketable housing financing credit instruments have been introduced, housing still has to give way when push comes to shove during periods of limited credit availability.

As Chart 17 indicates, new housing starts fall sharply whenever interest rates rise to high levels, but then recover when rates fall back. The cyclical behavior of housing activity has not been overcome by either governmental assistance or market innovation.

All that has happened is that mortgage-seeking borrowers have been given the opportunity to bid for funds during tight markets, something that was more difficult to do when markets were more regulated because home financing institutions—such as savings and loan associations and savings banks—used to simply run out of funds (due to depositor withdrawals) and that was that. The offsetting cost of this opportunity, however, has been a ratcheting up of the cost of money to everyone, including home buyers.

In addition, through credit flow analysis one can clearly fol-

Chart 16. External Financing Needs of Nonfinancial Corporations (Dollars in Billions) versus the Prime Lending Rate, 1966–85

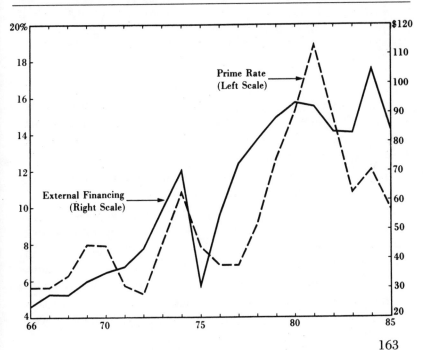

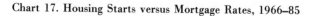

Chart 17. Housing Starts versus Mortgage Rates, 1966–85

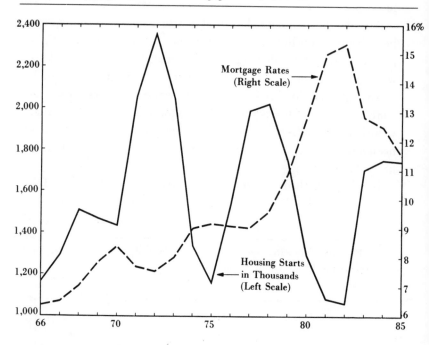

low the dynamic behavior of individual financial institutions as well as of groups of institutions. Consider the depiction in Chart 18 of the volatile growth typical of deposit-type institutions versus the more stable growth pattern that is shown for contractual savings institutions (encompassing life insurance companies, pension funds, and retirement funds).

The startling growth of money market mutual funds and the implications of their growth for market developments, policy responses, and financial regulation was evident quite early—in the mid-seventies—to credit flow analysts. Among other things, this growth made many savers sensitive for virtually the first time to interest-rate developments and to alternative investment opportunities. It also led to further liberalization of

Chart 18. Net Financial Asset Growth of Depository Institutions versus Contractual Savings, 1966–85 (Dollars in Billions)

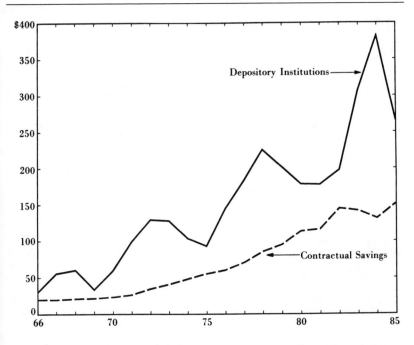

interest-rate ceilings on deposits and eventually to their complete removal.

Finally, the analysis of funds flows is also helpful in spotting shifts in the portfolio preferences of institutional investors. Some of these are cyclical and some are not; the credit flow analyst can readily discern the difference. Here are three examples:

1. Commercial bank investment in securities is not constant. Banks build up their securities holdings during recessions and early business recoveries, when loan demand is generally rather weak and monetary policy is accommodating. They then liquidate their securities as recovery progresses, when loan demand

165

Chart 19. Net Changes in Commercial Bank Investments and Loans, 1966–85 (Dollars in Billions)

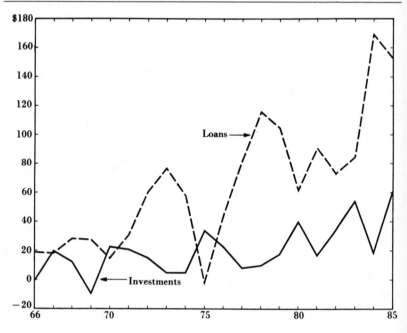

strengthens but monetary policy tightens (see Chart 19). This is one way in which one can observe the influence of monetary policy.

2. The municipal bond market, once an institutional market heavily dominated by commercial banks and to a lesser extent by fire and casualty insurance companies, has evolved to the point where these institutions now play a much smaller role than they did a decade or so ago. Household savings channeled through tax-exempt mutual funds and unit investment trusts are taking up most of this slack. As shown in Chart 20, the traditional institutional group that bought all of the net issuance of municipals during several years in the early seventies bought

Chart 20. Municipal Bond Purchases by Type of Investor, 1966–85 (Dollars in Billions)

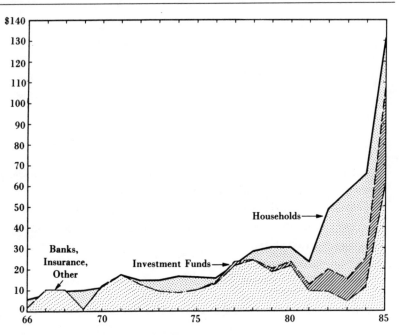

only 27 percent in 1984. This reflects, among other things, changes in portfolio strategies by these institutions, especially by banks. In contrast, tax-exempt mutual funds and unit invest-ment trusts purchased 47 percent of net municipal issuance in 1984.

3. As Table 15 shows, an extraordinary shift has taken place in the portfolio strategy of pension funds. In the sixties and early seventies, they invested most of their net new invest-ible funds in the stock market, but with subsequent increases in interest rates gradually and irregularly shifted a high pro-portion of these funds into fixed-income obligations. As a con-sequence, the equity market lost strong institutional support,

167

Table 15. Average Annual Net New Investible Funds of Private Pension
Funds (Dollars in Billions)

	1966–70	*1971–75*	*1976–80*	*1981–85*
Equities	$4.56	$ 6.28	$ 8.32	$ 9.48
Debt	1.34	7.74	21.53	26.80
Miscellaneous	0.74	1.45	2.20	1.38
Total	$6.64	$15.47	$32.05	$37.66
Equities as Percentage of Total	69%	41%	26%	25%

showing the pull of attractive interest rates. In recent years,
this slackening demand for equities by pension funds has been
offset in the market by larger investments by state and local
government retirement funds, mutual funds, and occasionally
by foreign investors.

CHAPTER 14

New Interest - Rate Precepts

The financial system used to be guided by tradition. Institutions had well-defined responsibilities, and excesses were rare. The consistency of ebb and flow in credit markets provided a refuge for analysis and decision making. In only a couple of decades, however, these conventions have vanished, with profound effects on interest rates.

Attitudes of borrowers, investors, and national policy-makers toward interest rates have changed drastically. We react to, and anticipate, interest-rate movements much more quickly than in the past. Out of all this, new interest-rate precepts have emerged, which must be understood if the management of money is to be up to date.

169

Interest Rates

Precept 1: The perception of high and low interest rates does not remain constant.

These days, yields of around 10 percent on high-grade long-term taxable bonds are considered on the low side, which is startling. Until recently, in the entire postwar era there have rarely been periods when double-digit interest prevailed for high-quality taxable issues.

The interest-rate perspectives of market participants are much influenced by previous cyclical rate peaks. These peaks in the latest cycle were about 15¼ percent for long Governments, 18½ percent for high-grade utilities, and about the same for mortgages. There is no permanent or absolute perception of what "high" and "low" yields are. Today, a home buyer regards 10 percent to 11½ percent as a most attractive financing cost and 14 percent to 15 percent as high. Both would have been unthinkable a decade ago.

Precept 2: Substantial interest-rate volatility is here to stay and should be incorporated into portfolio and financing decision making.

This new hallmark of the bond market has burst onto the scene with rather dramatic suddenness. I don't want to dwell on those stately days of the early sixties, when bill yields typically fluctuated 5 to 10 basis points a week and bond prices rose or fell by a quarter of a point. The change between 1974 and 1984 makes the point quite adequately.

As Table 16 indicates, from January 1974 through September 1979 the mean weekly price fluctuation of long Government bonds ranged from .49 percent to .66 percent. On the other hand, during the period October 1979 through 1982, when the Federal Reserve pursued a monetarist-oriented policy, the mean weekly price swing was 2.27 percent—three times as large as earlier. Alternatively stated, the standard deviation of changes in long bond prices climbed from .42 percent in 1974 to 1.20

percent during 1979–82—three times as large. Subsequently, after the Fed abandoned strict monetarism, volatility diminished but not to pre-1979 levels.

The new interest-rate volatility is here to stay. It takes larger movements in rates today to achieve the same results as were achieved in the past with smaller rate changes because of the increased role of expectations, because of the prevalence of floating rates, and because borrowers, lenders, and financial intermediaries all have more alternatives than they did before. Should the Fed return to monetarism, rate movements will be even more exaggerated.

Precept 3: Bonds are bought more for their price appreciation potential than for their income protection.

I advance this new precept with much hesitancy, because in many respects it undermines the distinctiveness and merit of a bond as a credit instrument. I wish it were not so. The fact remains, however, that the attractiveness of the contractual income protection offered by a bond has been whittled away by the corrosive effects of inflation.

Table 16. Volatility of Various Financial Instruments
(Weekly Range—High versus Low—Based on Daily Close)

	Percentage Price Change					
	U.S. Government				S&P 500	
	Long		Medium		Stocks	
	Avg.	SD	Avg.	SD	Avg.	SD
Jan. 74 to Oct. 74	.66%	.42%	.52%	.34%	2.94%	1.51%
Oct. 74 to Jan. 77	.65	.43	.42	.34	2.98	1.25
Jan. 77 to Sept. 79	.49	.37	.34	.30	1.47	.74
Oct. 79 to 1982	2.27	1.20	1.49	0.89	2.16	1.17
1983	1.23	0.54	0.78	0.37	1.85	0.95
1984	1.43	0.81	1.07	0.65	1.78	1.09

SD = standard deviation

For many years, the certainty of bond income was the foundation of institutional portfolio management designed to meet actuarial requirements, liquidity needs, and traditional prudent standards. Bonds served these needs well during periods of relative price stability.

But of course the generally poor performance of bonds relative to other credit instruments since 1974 has not gone unnoticed. Each successive cyclical thrust to new highs in interest rates (and new lows in bond prices) has widened the negative gap between cost and market value of institutional long bond holdings. What was once prudent in portfolio management has thus contributed to the shrinking of realizable values of institutional bond holdings.

A consequence of high and volatile interest rates has been a rush to risk aversion and to minimize price risks in bonds. Another likely consequence is that the regulatory and accounting authorities will insist that more institutions mark their fixed investments to market. If so, this will strengthen the trend to buying bonds for their price appreciation potential and toward making portfolio decisions to avoid losses.

Another development that has encouraged portfolio managers to focus on near-term performance has been the proliferation of marketable obligations. The rapid growth of the federal debt has been largely concentrated in highly marketable issues. In corporate finance, commercial paper has risen rapidly and public offerings of bonds have expanded at the expense of bank loans and private placements. The securitization of mortgages has also contributed to the volume of outstanding marketable obligations. This marketability invites portfolio valuations and calculations of *total* rates of return (including price appreciation or depreciation), again encouraging investors to focus on near-term rather than long-term achievements.

The new heightened volatility in bond prices can of course

mean bond losses, which encourages risk aversion despite the income assurance bonds provide. On the other hand, an occasional upswing in bond prices focuses attention on capital *appreciation* and not on income assurance and stability of principal. Bonds have come to be seen as vehicles with which to make a quick "killing."

Precept 4: The U.S. Government market is the pricing pacesetter of the bond market.

In less than a decade, the Government securities market has become an awesome giant. To a large extent, this is due to the continuously large new cash needs of the federal government, which in the fifties and early sixties followed more prudent fiscal policies than it does today. As a consequence, the volume of publicly held U.S. Government debt has leaped from $235 billion in 1960 to $285 billion in 1970 to $715 billion in 1980 and to $1.5 trillion in 1985.

The increasing leadership role of Government issues manifests itself in a variety of ways. The homogeneity of the Government market stands in sharp contrast to the growing heterogeneity of the corporate bond market. In addition, the size of individual Government issues dwarfs those of corporates. And while Government securities are, of course, of the highest credit caliber, the credit quality of corporate bonds has been slipping in recent years (see Table 17).

The result has been increasing perfection within Governments and the emergence of major differences within corporates. Yield spread analysis within Governments has validity, while running the risk of discontinuity within corporates. Today, the highest quality new corporate bond issue is priced right from the Government yield curve; issues of lesser quality, on the other hand, have no strong anchor. When you ask a corporate bond trader, "How is your market doing?" he responds by quoting price changes in long Governments.

Table 17. Profiles of Gross New Publicly Offered Corporate Bonds (Dollars in Billions)

	1977	1978	1979	1980	1981	1982	1983	1984
Total Public Corporate Bond Volume	$22.0	$17.5	$24.0	$34.0	$33.6	$42.3	$43.0	$63
Maturity Distribution								
Medium-term (less than 20 years)	16%	21%	30%	44%	55%	71%	59%	84%
Long-term (over 20 years)	84	79	70	56	45	29	41	16
Type								
Straight								
Conventional	96%	98%	89%	87%	73%	78%	65%	66%
Adjustable Rate	0	0	8	2	1	8	13	22
OID	0	0	0	0	13	8	8	6
Convertible	4	2	3	11	13	6	14	6
Quality Distribution								
Aaa	40%	29%	38%	25%	21%	4%	3%	1%
Aa	24	28	22	27	21	38	31	33
A	22	25	26	36	36	32	25	31
Baa	9	9	8	7	12	15	19	8
Unrated and Lower	5	9	6	5	10	11	22	27

Precept 5: Mortgage securities are alternatives to bonds, especially to corporate bonds.

For a long time, a dichotomy existed between the mortgage and bond markets. The former consisted of local and regional lender-borrowers dominated by a direct relationship between the two. Bonds were national and generally liquid credit instruments attracting a wide range of participants. Today, these structural arrangements are no more. Mortgage packages, securitized pools of mortgages, are rapidly becoming securities instruments competing in the national marketplace for funds.

In 1983, the securitization of the mortgage market was spurred by the introduction of mortgage-backed bonds that offer investors greater certainty of cash flow through the implementation of several maturity classes by the removal of Federal Housing Administration interest-rate ceilings and by the increasing acceptance of adjustable-rate mortgages.

New securitized mortgage loans have increased sharply as a proportion of 1–4 family mortgage originations, to an annual average of 25 percent over the three years 1982–84 compared with 14 percent during the previous five years (see Table 18).

The volume of new securitized mortgages has grown to exceed the gross issuance of new corporate bonds, and secondary market activity in mortgage securities has surpassed that in the corporate bond market. Mortgage securities are also turning in good total rates of return relative to other key markets—a development that obviously has helped lure investors to this market.

For example, mortgage securities in 1983 and 1984 recorded an average total rate of return of 13 percent compared with 11 percent for high-grade corporate bonds and 10 percent for medium-maturity Governments. Current coupon GNMA issues (fully guaranteed by the U.S. Government) have rather consistently yielded more than AA-rated utility bonds (see Chart 21).

In evaluating the implications of these developments for interest rates, it is important to focus on the changing position of

Table 18. Mortgage Loan Originations and Dollar Amount Securitized, 1970–84 (1–4 Family Loans, Dollars in Billions)

Year	Originations	New Loans Securitized	Ratio of New Loans Securitized to Originations
1970	$ 35.6	$ 0.5	1.4%
1971	57.8	2.8	4.8
1972	75.9	2.9	3.8
1973	79.1	2.9	3.7
1974	67.5	4.4	6.5
1975	77.9	7.8	10.0
1976	112.8	14.6	12.9
1977	162.0	21.4	13.2
1978	185.0	21.1	11.4
1979	187.0	28.4	15.2
1980	133.8	22.6	16.9
1981	98.2	14.4	14.7
1982	94.9	19.9	21.0
1983	201.9	70.0	34.7
1984	203.7	39.8	19.5

the mortgage borrower. The transfer of the mortgage into a securities form includes not only private obligations but also many Government-guaranteed and -sponsored organizations. The effectiveness of the mortgage demander has been enhanced through the offerings of housing bonds by state and local housing authorities, which in 1984 accounted for 19 percent of all municipal offerings as compared with 5 percent in 1977.

The mortgage market has, therefore, become more uniform than it was a few decades ago, while the corporate bond market has lost some of its homogeneity. Compared with bonds, many mortgage securities have larger and quicker cash flow schedules and offer variable interest rates to lenders—a great benefit to investors in an economy with an inflationary bias.

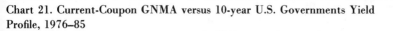

Chart 21. Current-Coupon GNMA versus 10-year U.S. Governments Yield
Profile, 1976–85

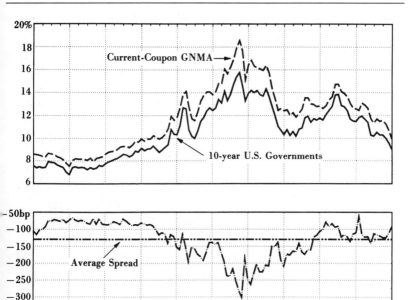

*Precept 6: Financial futures will continue to be an integral part
of interest-rate strategy.*

One can only conjecture at this time as to what extent financial
futures will permanently alter the financial landscape in the
United States. But the impact so far has been extraordinary. The
volume of trading in futures has grown to exceed that of cash
markets in certain key sectors, most notably in the long-term
bond market (see, for example, Chart 22).

The merits of financial futures are controversial. Unquestion-
ably, without financial futures it would have been very difficult
to underwrite the record volume of new bond offerings in recent

177

Chart 22. Volume of Transactions in Treasury Bonds Cash versus Futures, 1977–85 (Daily Averages, Dollars in Billions)

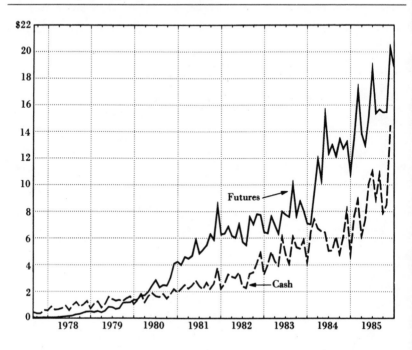

years. Futures, through intricate hedging operations, can reduce the underwriting risks inherent in extremely volatile markets. However, they have also enhanced the dominance of Government securities because futures are most applicable in homogeneous huge markets, a prerequisite amply met by Governments.

Futures also convert part of the traditional fixed-interest investment flows into commodity-type transactions, some of which have none of the savings-investment characteristics that underlie money flows into the securities markets. It is reasonable to assume that some of the individual participation in futures in recent years would have gone into traditional securities had futures not existed. Thus some funds were probably diverted from the saving-investment process.

Be that as it may, futures are here to stay. They will remain an important component of interest-rate strategy and serve, in some instances, as bond substitutes.

Precept 7: Interest rates in the United States are increasingly linked internationally.

While there always has been some link between U.S. and foreign interest rates, our sensitivity to developments abroad has soared.

In the seventies, the demise of the Bretton Woods Agreement led to the floating exchange rate system and to greater dependence on market forces, including interest rates, to adjust disequilibria in international payments. At the same time, the first oil shock of 1973/74 created massive imbalances in international payment flows, forcing the major oil importing countries, including the United States, to attract capital inflows to offset their rapidly deteriorating trade balances.

Thereafter, several other developments confirmed the international linkage of American interest rates. For example, the period of great dollar weakness, beginning in late 1976 and reaching its zenith in late 1979, was an important factor contributing to the Federal Reserve's adoption of a monetarist stance as it tightened monetary policy and drove interest rates up. The Fed moderated this stance in 1982, when the economy failed to revive and key developing countries were experiencing heavy debt burdens reflecting both their internal mismanagement and the high cost of borrowing in U.S. dollars.

The high level of interest rates in the United States during the years 1983 to 1985 helped attract huge sums of foreign funds to American shores, with foreign investments rising by a record $100 billion net in 1984. As of year-end 1984, foreigners held $750 billion of U.S. financial assets. Dollar weakness would induce many foreign investors to liquidate U.S. obligations and invest the proceeds elsewhere.

Opportunities to invest in other countries have increased markedly. Overall, in 1984 U.S. dollar-denominated bonds accounted for just over half of all bonds outstanding in the top thirteen currencies. In other words, the other twelve markets combined—Japan, West Germany, Italy, the United Kingdom, Canada, France, Belgium, Sweden, Denmark, Switzerland, Holland, and Australia—were about as large as the bond market (for all types of bonds) in the United States.

The growth of foreign bond markets has provided investors an opportunity to improve their overall rates of return. The performance of some of these markets has at times been superior to the American bond market. For example, from 1972 through 1979 an American investor would have been better off investing in money and bond obligations denominated in Swiss francs, Dutch guilders, French francs, deutsche marks, yen, and sterling than in U.S. dollars. A diversified investment in those six foreign markets would have annually increased portfolio performance over a strict U.S. dollar investment by 600 basis points for money market obligations and 860 basis points for bonds.

From 1978 through 1984, these opportunities have been varied. There were wide dispersions among the major markets and the United States ranked first in only one year (see Table 19).

CONCLUSION

These seven precepts of interest rates represent, in the main, a departure from the traditional litany. A few decades ago, a discussion of this subject would have stressed such "basics" as interest-rate stability, the merits of call protection, the value of contractual interest payments, the high quality of private debt, and historical interest rate relationships. To return to this era would require the imposition of economic disciplines far beyond

Table 19. Dispersion of Annual Total Returns in Major Government Bond Markets (Maturities Five Years and Over, Returns Measured in U.S. Dollars)

Market	1978	1979	1980	1981	1982	1983	1984
United States	−0.1%	1.9%	−0.8%	4.0%	31.3%	4.1%	14.3%H
Canada	−5.5L	−0.6	1.7	−2.4	35.8H	9.5	8.8
West Germany	16.2	7.3	−10.6L	−8.4	24.2	−7.7	−1.0
Japan	31.8	−21.5L	22.9	5.5H	3.3	12.6H	2.7
United Kingdom	3.2	12.4H	28.9H	−18.9L	26.4	1.1	−13.1
Switzerland	34.7H	−0.6	−9.6	−1.6	1.2L	−4.8	−14.6L
Netherlands	22.1	6.8	−5.8	−8.5	15.8	−8.6L	−2.6
France	31.1	0.1	−8.1	−16.0	1.9	−2.8	1.5
Dispersion:							
Highest less Lowest	40.2%	33.9%	39.5%	24.4%	34.6%	21.2%	28.9%

anything that is discernible today. In the meantime, fixed-income portfolio management must struggle to gain new footings because the traditional analytical framework is being shattered by excesses in the real world.

PART IV

The
Financial
Future

CHAPTER 15

Basic Forces Underlying the Investment Climate

Beginning with this chapter, I would like to try to peer into the murky depths of the financial future. I say murky because there has never before been such a vast amount of change in financial institutions and markets. Few institutions or markets look anything like they looked only a few years ago, and it is obvious that the process of change has a long way to go before it comes close to running its course. Of course, some metamorphosis is *always* occurring, but even so the transformation of financial markets and institutions in recent years has to be considered extraordinary.

To begin at the beginning, what are the conditions that should exist so that we have a cloudless financial horizon and profitable investments in the future? Most basic of all, and for that very reason usually overlooked, is a world at peace, at least with respect to the major powers and with respect to nuclear weapons. An armed confrontation between the superpowers would not only cause untold human suffering in terms of death, injury, and disease, which would be terrible enough, but would of course also devastate the financial landscape.

The state of the economy, a somewhat more complicated subject, is the second condition. Although some favor an over-heated economy as a source of investment gains, I think the past two decades prove that this is temporary and shortsighted. Over-heated economies are characterized by supply-and-demand dis-locations, wage-cost pressures, and especially by inflation, none of which favor profits or stock prices.

Far better for investment purposes is economic moderation—moderate growth, moderate unemployment, some unused physical resources, and price stability. If complete price stability has become an unrealizable goal, as the evidence of the past quarter century suggests, then at least we should hope for no more than moderate inflation—say, inflation at the pace of no more than 3 percent or so annually. Such a setting would foster a normal rate of economic growth—*real* economic growth—plus some occasional acceleration, without continuously bumping into economic and financial ceilings.

Under these circumstances, the financing of our economic requirements would pose few problems for the monetary authorities. There should be no difficulty staying within reasonable money and credit guidelines, and interest rates should be relatively low and fairly stable. To these blessings, we might also add domestic political and social stability, which Americans generally take for granted.

Looking back, we have never had a period of time in the post–World War II years during which all of these ideal conditions prevailed. Always, one or more of them has been lacking. Immediately following the war, we went through the war's inflationary aftermath, adjustment to a peacetime economy, a lengthy period of worldwide dollar shortage, and the problems of fiscal and monetary management in a new peacetime environment. The Federal Reserve and the U.S. Treasury had a difficult time learning to live together in an environment in which the two coexisted as equals; after all, during much of the forties the Federal Reserve was subordinated to the Treasury in the interest of the war effort and it was not easy to restore the Fed to an independent status upon the cessation of hostilities. It took until 1951, six years after the war's end, before the Treasury and Fed could get along together once again.

There was also the Cold War with the Soviet Union, the hot wars in Korea in the early fifties and Vietnam in the sixties, and repeated episodes throughout the world, especially in the Near East, that threatened to erupt into full-scale worldwide conflagrations.

Perhaps the nearest we came to an optimum investment climate was in the early sixties, say 1962–63, even though United States–Soviet relations were extremely tenuous at that time. But by 1962–63 the economy had fully recovered from recession, the unemployment rate was around 5 percent, and plant utilization in manufacturing slightly above 80 percent. Consumer prices rose only 1.2 percent in 1962 and 1.6 percent in 1963. The trend in wholesale commodity prices had been virtually flat since 1958. As for interest rates, Treasury bills were about 3 percent and long Governments about 4 percent. The Bretton Woods fixed-rate international monetary system was firmly in place and the dollar still strong around the world, although admittedly showing some signs of weakness. (Shortly thereafter, of course, everything unfortunately began to fall apart, with the assassination of President John F. Kennedy on November 22, 1963, the heating up of the Vietnam conflict a few years later, and the Watergate scandal in the early seventies.)

Present-day conditions are a substantial departure from optimum in terms of an investment environment. Interest rates are high, especially "real" rates. Our international trade imbalance is a cause for concern (in 1962 and 1963 we ran a $5 billion *surplus* each year in our goods and services balance of international payments). Our manufacturing and agricultural sectors are under pressure. And the federal budget deficit, which was around $5 billion in 1962 and 1963, is *forty* times that today although GNP is only seven or eight times larger than it was in 1962–63.

Given the circumstances, it is easy to be swayed by the immediate event and to underestimate the importance of long-term forces that exert a profound undertow on the investment climate.

INTERNATIONAL COOPERATION

In the post–World War II era, immense strides have been made in bringing the people of the world closer together through technological, political, and economic means. How far we have come can be judged if one thinks back to the days of Adolf Hitler, the worldwide Great Depression of the thirties, the feudal times of Europe, or even to the days of Alexander the Great, and ponders whether there was a greater feeling of hope then or now for man to break his bondage to misery and ignorance. Clearly, there is greater hope today than in the past.

We live in an age of nuclear tension. Nevertheless, twenty years after World War I the world was on the brink of another eruption, another world war. Forty years have now passed since the end of World War II and while there have been numerous limited wars, a worldwide struggle has not taken place. It appears as though the ultimate weapons, atomic and hydrogen bombs, may actually have become deterrents rather than incitements to aggression.

Progress toward one world is probably most visible in transportation and communications. Hardly a spot is left on earth that is not readily accessible or within range of telephone, radio, or television. Travel has become a growth industry, and escape places for the venturesome increasingly difficult to find.

World integration has also been assisted by regional cooperation along the lines of the Common Market, by the tremendous expansion since the end of World War II of multinational corporations, and by the relative stability of the international financial system. The Bretton Woods system of fixed exchange rates based on gold has broken down and been replaced by floating exchange rates based on supply and demand, but the International Monetary Fund and the World Bank—creatures of Bretton Woods—remain and even flourish on the international scene. And everything considered the international financial system is a vast improvement over developments in the twenties and thirties, when beggar-thy-neighbor policies in the form of exchange restrictions and tariffs produced an eventual contraction in world trade.

THE EFFECTIVENESS OF SOCIAL DEMANDS

The past several decades have also witnessed a vast awakening to social demands, a sensitivity that may be unique in the history of the world. It is not that the need to alleviate poverty and to improve health, education, and opportunity were not there previously, but rather that these needs attained political expression for the first time.

In the past quarter century, many social aspirations have become realities. Many others are still awaiting fulfillment and new ones have emerged as rapidly as existing ones have been satisfied. In the United States, and in many western European countries also, as well as in Canada and elsewhere, the response of government to these aspirations has had a powerful influence on the investment climate. It has virtually eliminated fears of another major depression, for example, but at the same time may have contributed to the likelihood of chronic inflation.

A NEW POPULATION

Another powerful force underlying the investment environment is our new population, namely, the increasing number of young people entering the labor force. Their backgrounds, skills, and ambitions are in many ways different from young entrants into the labor force several decades ago.

Reared in the post-Depression era, this young population possesses none of the economic fears with respect to security and safety that were so evident in earlier generations. Consequently, their traits differ, both off and on the job. They spend freely, for instance, and at an early stage in their adult life, and they do not generally have a strong feeling about our Puritan heritage; indeed, it is practically absent.

Benjamin Franklin's saying "Who goeth a borrowing goeth a sorrowing" does not apply to them. Generally, our new population has allocated a high percentage of earnings to debt service and has relied more on contractual than on discretionary savings for providing funds for potential emergencies. The fact that many are two-wage-earner families, because of the entrance of women into the labor force, contributes to and reinforces these attitudes.

On the job, an important characteristic of this new population is its drive to implement aggressive economic and financial decisions when given the opportunity. The increasing emphasis on performance in portfolio management is the result of the initiative and prodding of the young. The conglomerate movement was similarly given added momentum by them, both in financial institutions and in business corporations. It is no surprise to find younger people frequently dominating the rapidly growing new sectors of our economy—computer technology is a prime example—while the policies of stable and traditional industries, and of labor unions, too, for that matter, are still set by an older generation.

What is the significance of this new population to the future investment climate? There are too many ramifications to discuss them all, from their propensities with regard to having children to the frozen food quick-dinner industry, from their vacation wishes to their work habits. To mention just a few observations, their spending will probably increase and so will their reliance on contractual savings.

Moreover, the new generation is already and will continue to be better educated and more highly trained and skilled than previous generations. Consequently, as they enter the work force, they will continue to ask for and indeed will be entitled to relatively high starting salaries and wages, which will permit them to embark on a fairly high standard of living from the beginning. They will also be employed in less cyclical occupations, which will additionally enhance their credit worthiness. From an investment viewpoint, it is interesting to speculate on what will happen when leadership of the traditional and stable businesses is relinquished to the young. Their aggressive and innovative drive may bring about many alterations in old-fashioned ways of doing things.

One frequently overlooked element in the new population is the growing influence of minorities and the underprivileged. As we strive to overcome our bigotry, blacks and other oppressed minority groups will enter the mainstream of the economy in ever-increasing numbers. Their educational background and skills are on the upgrade, bringing them into better jobs and positions of increasing authority.

As a result, this newly emerging group will also start moving up to a higher standard of living. Its demands for goods and services will change in character as well as quantity. The ghetto dweller of today will be the home buyer and two-car family of the future; in other words, many of America's social problems today will produce its opportunities of tomorrow. Meeting these challenges will strengthen both the economy and the democratic nature of our society.

TECHNOLOGICAL PROGRESS

Technological change is the most prominent and dramatic feature of the twentieth century. Technological innovations thus far in this century are unparalleled in the history of mankind. We differ from the past in that we incorporate technological change into our planning, our thinking, our decision making, and we confidently anticipate further technological improvements in virtually every sphere of business activity. Contributing to this optimism is not only talk but evidence of a new leisure class and a post-industrial society.

Our rapid industrial strides are laying to rest one of the deepest-seated and longest-lived fears regarding technological change, namely, worry about technological unemployment. The concern has been misplaced all along, because innovations and new processes generate new services and new products and with them the demand for new skills and additional labor. Actually, in many ways labor is in a more advantageous bargaining position in a highly mechanized and computerized business than in an industry still heavily dependent on manual labor.

Technology implies another change: the wealth of nations can no longer be judged merely by their natural wealth and resources or their total population. The skill of its people is becoming an increasingly important determinant of a nation's wealth, especially as industrial activity diminishes in relative importance and secondary activities gain in significance.

Perhaps real wealth will be increasingly identified with knowledge. If so, a new obsolescence will have to be dealt with in that skills will have to be continuously updated to maintain productivity. Periodic returns to classrooms to renew knowledge may eventually become mandatory if one hopes to move up the corporate ladder.

PLANNING

One of the important by-products of economic progress has been the advent of planning as part of an effective business program. Corporate long-range planning has been joined by product planning, strategic investment planning, and market planning ranging in scope from local to international. Although not all plans materialize, plans play an important role in helping to define and clarify alternatives and outline different ways of achieving various objectives. They also contribute to business optimism and thereby strengthen the investment environment.

However, because of the increasing popularity of planning in the business community, financial and economic analysts are placed in the difficult position of having to evaluate the accuracy and reasonableness of corporate sales-and-profit projections that involve implicit assumptions and computer simulations. Accurate evaluations of ones's own plans are difficult enough, not to mention evaluating plans drawn up by others.

Despite the prevalence of business planning, we still have not developed adequate techniques for assessing the real risks involved in embarking on new programs. Unfortunately, there are no future facts, only past ones. For example, it has become highly fashionable to install new plant and equipment in order to replace labor with machinery, to automate, and to produce larger quantities.

To a large extent, these decisions are undertaken in order to escape rising labor costs, especially in industries where unions are strongly entrenched. However, such decisions often neglect the risk of obsolescence. With technological change a permanent and growing feature of the modern economy, and with intense international competition, which disperses technological change originating abroad as well as at home, obsolescence can be expected to accelerate.

This has long been a recognized problem in the area of military procurement, where weapons systems go out of date almost before the ink is dry on contracts ordering their production, but it is now becoming almost as important in business in general. This means that incorrect planning decisions regarding the installation of technology can have a much more dramatic adverse impact on profits than did the scuttling of a labor assembly line. The planning lead time in an advanced industrial economy tends to be long, thereby enhancing risk in the capitalization of research-and-development expenditures and in the acquisition of expensive new high-tech capital equipment.

Of course, planning—including the defining of objectives and the allocation of resources—has not been adopted by all sectors of the economy. Its popularity in the United States lies in the *private* sector, especially in the business community. This is in contrast to totalitarian countries, where planning is the plaything of governments; totalitarian bureaucracies spend much of their time enunciating short- and long-range plans, popularizing slogans regarding them, slogans with public relations appeal, and whipping up public enthusiasm.

The fact that governmental planning is identified with totalitarian countries has given it such a bad name that many capitalist democracies tend to avoid even the appearance of planning. This is unfortunate, because planning does not have to fit the totalitarian mold. It can show alternatives instead of issuing orders. The lack of even intermediate planning by our federal government has often had a destabilizing influence on the economy.

THE INSTITUTIONALIZATION OF SAVING AND INVESTMENT

One of the most significant recent developments has been the increasing institutionalization of saving and investment. That is, most personal saving used to result from households deciding to consume somewhat less; once that decision was made, savers tended to use their saved funds to directly buy stocks or bonds for their own portfolios.

The growing institutionalization of saving and investment is indicated in Table 20, which shows the diminishing share of saving that is invested directly by households on their own, and the increasing share that is invested through the facilities of financial intermediaries of one sort or another. The intermediated flows include savings allocated to insurance and pension reserves, funds that are invested by money market and other mutual funds, and deposits placed in banks and thrift institutions.

New intermediated savings averaged an estimated $58 billion annually in the five years ended 1970. During the next ten years household savings naturally grew in absolute terms, but they remained rather constant with respect to the proportion intermediated through financial institutions. However, with interest rate deregulation and other developments, in the years 1981–85 household intermediated savings expanded at the expense of direct investments.

One element that has contributed to the growth of intermediated savings and investments has been the deregulation of financial institutions, especially with respect to interest payments on time and savings deposits. This began in the early

Table 20. Net New Household Savings and Their Disposition
(Annual Averages; Dollars in Billions)

Years	Total	Intermediated	Direct	Intermediated as Percent of Total
1966–70	$ 67.9	$ 57.9	$10.0	85%
1971–75	138.4	120.2	18.2	87
1976–80	259.4	222.7	36.7	86
1981–85	422.0	395.9	26.1	94

sixties, when commercial banks were first permitted to issue large-size negotiable certificates of deposit. It was further encouraged in the seventies with the introduction of money market mutual funds and then the gradual elimination of deposit-rate ceilings. In recent years, the trend has been given impetus by such legislation as the 1980 Depository Institutions Deregulation and Monetary Control Act and the 1982 Garn–St. Germain Act, which broadened the powers of thrift institutions.

While the institutionalization of savings has helped to spawn new credit instruments and trading techniques, it has also complicated the task of monetary management. As I noted earlier, the removal of interest-rate ceilings on deposits gives deposit institutions the opportunity to maintain growth objectives that contradict the objectives of the Federal Reserve. The consequences have been increased interest-rate volatility and, in periods of credit restraint, higher rate levels than would otherwise prevail. These are all important influences to take into consideration when formulating investment strategies.

CHAPTER 16

Credit Markets in 1995

It would be folly to think that financial change has come to an end, or even that its pace is likely to slow. There is nothing in the fundamental behavior of the economy, the attitudes and practices of market participants, the likely course of national or international policies, or the history of science and technology that would suggest a slowing of the rate of change.

Indeed, quite the contrary. The more change occurs the more it feeds upon itself and cumulates. This chapter sketches some of the dimensions that I believe will characterize the American credit/debt market a decade from now. (Since everyone's debt is someone else's credit, because it is impossible to borrow without a lender to provide the funds, "credit market" and "debt market" are used virtually interchangeably.)

197

SIZE OF THE MARKET

Naturally enough, by a decade from now the American credit market will be much larger than it is at the present time. Two forces will propel this growth: (1) growth in our nominal gross national product, probably at the rate of 5 percent to 10 percent per annum (the specific amount depending largely on the rate of inflation that occurs); and (2) the extent to which our credit structure continues to be leveraged through debt financing. Earlier, I pointed out the correlation between the level of GNP and credit market debt—how close this linkage was in the early postwar years and how much more rapidly debt has increased relative to GNP in the past five years.

Even a wide range of assumptions for underlying economic expansion and concomitant credit growth will produce a credit market of formidable size by 1995. A rate of debt growth comparable to that of the sixties would mean a credit market approximately $16 trillion in size by 1995 as compared with $8 trillion at the end of 1985. A rate of debt growth comparable to the seventies, on the other hand, would mean a credit market approximately $19 trillion in size by 1995 (see Table 21).

Although the torrid pace of debt growth in the first half of the eighties may not continue, neither is the moderate pace of the early sixties likely to return, for several reasons.

For one, there is no indication that the rate of inflation, which is an important component of nominal GNP growth and thus a determinant of debt growth, will return to the low levels that prevailed in the late fifties and early sixties. From 1955 to 1965, the inflation rate averaged 1.6 percent per annum (which was considered a cause for concern!).

Much of the deceleration in the rate of inflation in the early eighties was due to the sluggish pace of economic expansion outside the United States and to the large availability of unused resources both in the United States and abroad. In addition, the extraordinary strength of the dollar on foreign exchange mar-

Table 21. Growth of U.S. Credit Market Debt and Nominal Gross National Product

Five Years Ending	Growth Rate of:		Size of Credit Market (end of period) (Dollars in Billions)
	GNP	Debt	
1960	4.9%	6.7%	778
1965	6.4	8.4	1106
1970	7.5	8.9	1597
1975	9.3	12.8	2620
1980	11.2	15.4	4641
1985	8.2	14.3	7968
1995E[a]		8.5	14741
		10.0	15936
		14.0	19124

[a]E = estimated.

kets helped to hold down the U.S. inflation rate. It did so making foreign goods much cheaper for Americans to buy, thereby inhibiting U.S. producers from raising prices because of fear of losing sales to foreign competition; and also by reducing foreign demand for American-made products, which became priced out of the reach of foreigners because they had to pay so much of their own money to get dollars. An "overvalued" dollar is not likely to be a permanent feature of the economic landscape.

Second, our tax structure will probably continue to favor debt over equity finance even though tax reform may chip away here and there at the advantage held by bonds over stocks in raising corporate funds. It would require extraordinary political stamina to sharply curtail the tax deductibility benefits of interest payment costs and to encourage equity financing.

Third, the securitization of debt—the shift from nonmarketable to marketable debt—will continue and thus encourage new credit instruments and the creation of new debt. The intensity of financial innovation has not yet crested.

A more critical issue regarding the size of the credit market in 1995 involves deterioration in the quality of credit. Can debt continue to expand at a rapid pace in view of the decline in credit quality that has already occurred in key sectors at home and abroad? At first glance, one would conclude that debt growth will have to slow down because of quality considerations. A lower credit rating generally means greater difficulty borrowing. However, this conclusion is probably influenced by views regarding caution and prudence that were popular a generation or two ago but are no longer very widespread.

Closer inspection of the data suggests that there are still substantial segments of the financial system that have the potential for greater leveraging, albeit with increasing risk. For example, such capacity still resides in some corporations, large groups of households, and a variety of financial institutions, such as life insurance companies and medium and smaller-sized commercial banks. To exploit this capability may require new credit techniques and ingenuity, of which there seems to be no shortage.

For a more marginal credit/debt structure to survive will entail even more socialization of debt problems than we have seen to date. Such a trend is already visible. Neither large corporations nor large financial institutions have been permitted to fail—witness Lockheed (1971), Chrysler (1979), First Pennsylvania Bank (1980), and Continental Illinois Bank (1984).

Official financial safety nets seem to cover large corporations, banks, savings and loan associations, major insurance companies, and key developing countries. The more marginal the credit structure becomes, the more debt socialization will become visible along with federal government involvement in the management of financial institutions and markets.

In the Continental Illinois case, the federal government has in effect become a partner in the management of the institution; both the chairman of the board and the chief executive officer of the holding company and the chairman of the board and chief executive officer of the bank are federal government appointees.

The alternative to debt socialization is either to reregulate financial markets or to allow several major failures to take place as a means of disciplining the system. Reregulation at this time does not appear likely: the deregulation philosophy continues to dominate thinking in the United States and deregulation is accelerating in many other industrial countries as well.

Allowing major failures as a means of disciplining the system is no more practical than reregulation, perhaps even less so. In its 1984 *Annual Report* (page 4), the Federal Deposit Insurance Corporation explained in convincing fashion why permitting Continental Illinois to fail and paying off only insured depositors was never seriously considered an option:

> Insured accounts [in Continental Illinois] totalled only slightly more than $3 billion. This meant that uninsured depositors and other private creditors with over $30 billion in claims would have had their funds tied up for years in a bankruptcy proceeding awaiting the liquidation of assets and the settlement of litigation. Hundreds of small banks would have been particularly hard hit. Almost 2,300 small banks had nearly $6 billion at risk in Continental; 66 of them had more than their capital on the line and another 113 had between 50 and 100 percent.

THE MARKETPLACE

The sheer size of the market in 1995 will pose challenges to investment bankers and securities firms. To be sure, it is exciting to think that in ten years new corporate debt offerings will often total $1 billion to $2 billion, or that gross Treasury financing volume will be several times larger than it is today.

However, larger and more diverse markets will mean more complex value relationships, the creation of even more credit instruments and more frequent and much larger institutional portfolio adjustments to realign values. Linkages between markets here and abroad will multiply with improved computer and communications technology. More clerical services, including perhaps most of the processing of transactions, may be farmed out to specialists. Many more transactions will be on a book-entry basis, and the physical delivery of securities may have been eliminated for most major markets.

The securities trader of the nineties will be facing computerized screens that automatically show aberrations in value relationships, so that arbitraging transactions will be automatically indicated. Many transactions will be consummated through electronic trading systems that will be monitored by traders, but the traders themselves will get involved only in special cases.

Round-the-clock trading should be formalized well before 1995. It is already informally practiced today at securities firms where traders in the New York market are called in the middle of the night by their associates in the Far East. As these transactions become much larger, however, it will be difficult to say whether dealer inventories should be valued on the basis of "closing" prices in New York, London, or Tokyo.

From the viewpoint of financial theorists, the financial markets of the nineties will be more "perfect" than they are today, in terms of the widespread and rapid dissemination of knowledge and information and its prompt incorporation in securities prices. From the viewpoint of the marketplace, the advantages and disadvantages of financial near-perfection should be clearly understood.

As financial markets move increasingly toward perfection, barriers to money flows are reduced, traditions in finance involving noneconomic relationships are uprooted, and the sheer price of money becomes just about the sole determinant of transactions. Local and regional securities firms as well as other financial institutions will increasingly feel the pull of national and even international credit markets.

Today's few remaining pools of idle funds will be eliminated by 1995. Although only a few have done so to date, many more large business borrowers will bypass the underwriter with some of their new offerings. In general, profit margins of securities firms and of financial intermediaries should shrink somewhat. In some cases, this will be more than offset by the much larger volume of transactions. As in the past, this profit margin squeeze will encourage securities firms to seek new trading and financial opportunities with improved profit potential.

Within the next decade, securities firms will have to confront two potentially limiting forces. One is the changing nature of their business, from traditional trading and underwriting to somewhat more of a spread banking business. The other is the likelihood of increasing competition from other institutions.

The ballooning of spread banking activities by securities firms has been mainly due to the proliferation of marketable securities and of proxy credit instruments such as options and futures and the introduction of interest-rate and currency swaps. These have enabled investment banking houses to vastly increase their arbitrage and hedging operations, which in volatile financial markets have limited risks and can increase profits.

The dark side of this development is that there are few perfect arbitrage and hedging opportunities. Most opportunities involve some credit and maturity risks and the assumption that the market mechanism, particularly the clearing function, will operate without disruption.

Even more important, the spread banking activity of securities firms is rapidly enlarging their balance sheets. In many instances, balance-sheet and off-balance-sheet items are growing more rapidly than capital, while the maturity of the spread banking operations is being extended. This trend is bound to lead to greater financial disclosure requirements for securities firms and new standards for capital requirements.

The most pressing competitive issue facing securities firms is whether other institutions—particularly commercial banks—

will be allowed to underwrite and trade in corporate securities. At present, securities firms and the banks are locked in head-to-head combat over this issue.

The position of the securities industry is as follows:

1. Banks are unique financial institutions, entrusted with fiduciary responsibilities with respect to the acceptance of deposits and the creation of money that preclude their involvement in a business as risky as underwriting and trading in corporate securities. The unique nature of banks is the reason they have such special governmental privileges as federal deposit insurance, favorable tax treatment, and access to the Federal Reserve's discount facilities.

2. The public's confidence in the safety and stability of the banking system is already shaky, due to the large number of bank failures in recent years and the banks' well-known holdings of third-world loans that are unlikely to be repaid in the near future. Adding underwriting and trading in corporate issues to their activities would only erode public confidence in the safety of the banking system even further.

3. When banks were permitted to underwrite corporate securities, in the late twenties and early thirties, a number of abuses occurred that led to the passage of the Glass-Steagall Act in 1933, the legislation which separated commercial banking from investment banking. Among the most flagrant abuses was dumping unsold issues that banks had underwritten into trust funds that they managed. Such conflicts of interest would still exist today if banks were allowed to return to the underwriting business.

4. Bank allegations that the securities business is not competitive and is exceedingly profitable are false. Ease of entry and negotiated rates have led to an intensely competitive industry.

Moreover, profitability in the securities industry is much more volatile than in banking.

The commercial banking industry, of course, looks at repeal of the Glass-Steagall Act of 1933 rather differently. As the banking industry sees it:

1. Structural defects in the banking system and financial abuses that existed in the twenties and early thirties were corrected by the strengthening of the Federal Reserve, the creation of federal deposit insurance, and the regulation of the securities markets by the newly created Securities and Exchange Commission. The separation of investment banking from commercial banking in the Glass-Steagall Act was not necessary to achieve or maintain these reforms.

2. Potential conflicts of interest that may arise from underwriting or trading activities can be regulated in the same way that similar potential conflicts in both the banking system and the securities industry are regulated now.

3. More competition in the significantly concentrated securities industry would benefit small and large companies that use investment banking services, as well as individual and institutional investors.

The conflict between (a) bank efforts to get involved in underwriting and trading corporate securities and (b) the opposition of securities houses to those efforts, is unlikely to be resolved in the near future. In 1983, BankAmerica, one of the country's largest bank holding companies, acquired Charles J. Schwab & Company, the nation's largest discount broker. Other large commercial banks have followed suit, with their own acquisition or establishment of a discount brokerage function.

All of these were validated by the U.S. Supreme Court in

1984, when it ruled that such activities did not violate the Glass-Steagall Act. Also Security Pacific National Bank purchased a seat on the New York Stock Exchange in 1983, the first bank in over fifty years to do so directly—that is, without buying a company that already owned one.

Nevertheless, Congress and the courts are likely to stop well short of total repeal of the Glass-Steagall Act. That is, Congress and the courts are likely to keep a meaningful separation between investment and commercial banking, even though here and there the wall separating the two may give way somewhat.

This is because financial volatility and occasional turbulence will not permit commercial banks to strengthen their balance sheets sufficiently to encourage Congress to abrogate the Act. Further dismantling of Glass-Steagall may occur by 1995 if by then bank assets are more conservatively stated than they are now and particularly if all institutions are then operating on a somewhat more level playing field.

However, this would require considerable progress toward achieving uniform accounting standards for financial institutions, the reporting of assets at the lower of acquisition cost or current market value, and limiting the advantage presently accruing to banks from federal deposit insurance.

Meanwhile, some chipping away at Glass-Steagall through *de facto* market pressures is highly likely. That is, many of the changes that have been taking place in the financial system have occurred because aggressive financial institutions have skirted or bent the law; subsequently, Congress and the courts have validated what at first glance appeared to be illegal. A similar pattern of change is not unlikely, at least to some extent, with respect to the separation of commercial and investment banking.

U.S. TREASURY BORROWING

The U.S. Government securities market will remain the anchor of the American debt market in 1995. This market will continue to grow between now and 1995, although hardly at the extraordinary pace of the last few years, when from the end of 1980 to the end of 1985 federal government debt rose by $900 billion or 15 percent per annum on average. While many new initiatives to lower the size of the federal budget deficit are likely to be discussed in the next few years, none is likely to be in fact taken. Nevertheless, the size of the federal budget deficit relative to nominal gross national product (GNP) will probably fall.

The federal budget deficit as a percent of nominal GNP averaged 1.3 percent in the ten years ended in 1975, 2.4 percent in the five years ended in 1980, and 4.4 percent in the subsequent five years. To return to the relatively low percentage of the early years will require exceedingly rapid GNP growth, tax-rate increases, a further cutback in the growth of government spending, or some combination thereof.

For the foreseeable future, the American economy is not likely to generate real economic growth of more than 3 percent per annum for any extended period of time. An increase in tax rates of any significant amount is hardly ever legislated except in times of national emergency, such as war. There is virtually no chance that political leaders will support a peacetime tax-rate increase in the aftermath of the 1984 national elections, which was in part a referendum on that very issue. Democratic Party candidate Walter Mondale proposed a tax increase in order to reduce the federal deficit, and was roundly defeated for his efforts. It will be most surprising if anyone repeats that political strategy in the near future.

While some slowing in the growth of defense outlays between now and 1995 is a reasonable possibility, given the large buildup in recent years, a significant reversal in nonmilitary expenditures will require a major turnaround in the nation's social priorities. Although the electorate appears to be satisfied with less government spending than existed a few years ago, it is not at all clear that it wants less than it has today.

Consequently, in estimating the size of the U.S. Government

securities market in 1995 I have projected that nominal GNP will increase at an annual 8 percent rate between now and then and that the federal deficit will gradually work its way down to about 3 percent of (nominal) GNP. This implies that the volume of outstanding federal debt will be $3.7 trillion in 1995, which compares with $1.8 trillion at the end of 1985, $900 billion at the end of 1980, and $550 billion in 1975.

A better perspective on the dimensions of the Government securities market in 1995 can be gained from Table 22, which shows the likely composition of financing by type of obligation and maturity. For example, the weekly auctions of 3-month and 6-month Treasury bills may total $26 billion, up from $14 billion in 1985 and $7.6 billion in 1980. The mid-quarterly offerings of new Treasury coupon issues will be an estimated $43 billion as compared with $22 billion at the end of 1985.

Associated with this growth will also be more rapid growth in the volume of financial futures transactions in Government securities. This is partly because Government futures are used to offset risks in other markets—which of course will also in-

Table 22. Auction Sizes of U.S. Treasury Debt Offerings for Selected Fiscal Year-ends (Dollars in Billions)

	1980	1985	1995E[a]
3- and 6-month Bill	$7.60	$14.40	$26.00
1-year Bill	4.00	8.75	12.25
2-year Note	4.50	9.25	12.75
3-year Note	4.00	8.50	15.25
4-year Note	3.00	6.50	14.25
5-year Note	3.00	7.25	14.50
7-year Note	2.00	6.00	13.50
10-year Note	2.75	6.75	14.00
20-year Bond (15 yrs. in 1980)	1.50	4.50	12.25
30-year Bond	1.50	6.50	14.00

[a]E = estimated.

crease in size—and partly because additional futures and options securities will be innovated as segments of the Government market become deeper in size.

In any event, Governments will maintain their market leadership role as price-setters against which other markets will price their issues. This will be due to the large size of the Government securities market and, just as importantly, to its homogeneity in terms of yield and maturity characteristics and high quality.

CORPORATE FINANCE

A continuation of the irregular upward trend in the external financing of business corporations will be another by-product of economic growth from now to 1995. As shown in Chart 23, the jagged upward path of external financing has highly cyclical characteristics that are not likely to change appreciably in the future. External financing—that is financing from outside the firm, financing other than funds generated by depreciation and retained earnings—which in the five years ended in 1985 averaged annually about $88 billion, in 1995 may reach about $120 billion.

By 1995, however, the structure of the corporate financing market, and the market for outstanding corporate securities, will have undergone substantial changes. The traditional corporate bond market (namely, the market for long bonds) will have grown only modestly, at best, as the preference for floating-rate and medium maturity financing persists. Thus large continuing refinancing requirements, as securities keep maturing, will keep corporations substantial demanders of gross, if not net, new funds.

Unless interest rates fall further than expected, many low coupon corporate bonds will be retired in the nineties, bonds that first saw the light of day in the fifties. This will eliminate a tradable sector of the market.

In addition, at least one and perhaps two economic contrac-

Chart 23. External Financing Needs of Nonfinancial Corporations, 1960–85 (Dollars in Billions)

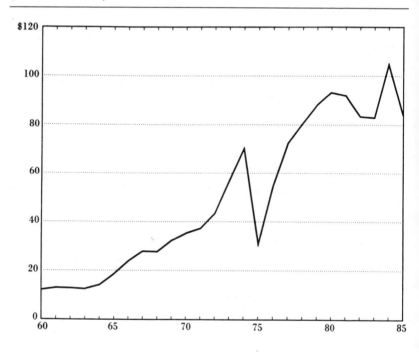

tions between now and 1995 will test the resiliency of the so-called "junk bond" market. The ensuing casualties are bound to increase the volume of new equity financing and probably give renewed impetus to mergers and consolidations.

By 1995, the use of interest-rate and currency swaps to facilitate borrowing arrangements will no doubt be circumscribed by the regulatory authorities and will not be as easily arranged as has been the case in recent years. There will be closer scrutiny of maturity and credit risk in this area.

There will probably be at least two troublesome developments in the corporate bond market. One will revolve around the heterogeneity of the market, since it consists of not-very-well-defined maturity and credit quality groups. Long maturity sectors will be relatively thin and shorter obligations will vary widely in credit quality and many will have custom-tailored financing provisions. These inconsistencies will make relative value analyses difficult, increase the need for effective credit appraisal, and slow the volume of secondary market trading. The other troublesome development in the market for corporate bonds will be stiffer competition from proliferating securitized obligations in other markets, obligations that heretofore have absorbed limited amounts of funds.

MUNICIPALS

The market for municipal securities is a candidate for startling changes over the coming decade. Substantial growth is only one of the elements involved. However, it is a significant element. Outstanding debt of state and local governments today totals $615 billion. In ten years, this market should be $1.4 trillion to $1.7 trillion in size assuming an 8 percent per annum growth in nominal GNP.

State and local government infrastructure needs that have been building up for many years can no longer be denied. In addition, many of our larger cities have experienced a rebirth in the last few years after having been virtually given up for dead. The infusion of private funds that has rebuilt whole neighborhoods requires more than ever that the urban infrastructure —roads, bridges, mass transportation, schools, fire and police protection—be modernized in support of the revitalization that appears to be underway.

There is also considerable room for improvement in the financing techniques currently practiced in this market. More smaller issuers may enlarge their borrowing power by issuing their obligations through state-sponsored banks, by purchasing bond insurance, or by marketing their securities through new private financing institutions that specialize in the obligations of small municipalities (and in turn finance themselves in the open market through bulk borrowings). In addition, the disallowance of industrial revenue financing through the tax-exempt route will encourage the establishment of taxable state-sponsored industrial development banks that, because they will be offering a taxable interest rate, will be able to sell their obligations extensively abroad as well as domestically.

The most profound change in this market, however, is likely to take place in the area of secondary market trading practices and in the management of municipal investments. At present, the bulk of market activity relates to new issues, while secondary market activity remains rather moderate. Individual investors have dominated the market, generally buying state and local obligations not to trade but to hold to maturity; they have thus forsaken a higher total return that potentially might have been obtained.

There are substantial opportunities for improving portfolio performance in the tax-exempt market. In addition, thus far relatively few portfolio managers have chosen to specialize in municipals, thereby providing an enticing opportunity for newcomers. The market is also shifting away from direct investment by individuals to the placing of funds in municipal mutual funds and unit investment trusts. Of all the investment grade markets, municipals may well offer the greatest growth opportunity for future professional portfolio managers.

HOUSEHOLD FINANCE

No end to the rapid rise in household debt seems in sight, even though household borrowing and leverage ratios are historically high. For example, the ratio of consumer credit outstanding to disposable personal income was at a record 19 percent in 1985 as compared with 15 percent in 1970.

Why will this trend continue? Fundamentally, it will continue because there is a greater willingness to accept debt by those

212

coming of age than used to be the case with previous generations. For previous generations, debt was a "bad" thing, to be
avoided or utilized only when there was no other alternative.
Those coming of age now do not view debt in that light; they
think of going into debt as a natural and normal way of conduct-
ing their financial affairs.

The present generation does not share the fear of economic
depression that haunted their parents. They know of depression
only from the history books. In their experience, inflation has
been the nagging economic problem, not mass unemployment,
and if money is expected to erode in purchasing power over time
then borrowing today and repaying tomorrow (in dollars of less
value) makes sense.

Many are also employed in service industries, which are less
cyclical than manufacturing, thereby encouraging them to leverage more. And often there are two wage earners in a family,
instead of one, an increasing trend that will probably foster
further liberalities in consumer and household borrowing. Such
borrowing will also become more automatic and less cumber-
some through the use of personal computers, which will facilitate not only the actual crediting and debiting arrangements but
also enable individuals to comparison shop through daily post-
ings of financing costs on video screens.

A further inducement to such borrowing will come from a
decline in its cost relative to interest costs charged other borrowers. Although consumers have traditionally paid relatively high
interest rates, and although these rates have traditionally been
rather sticky on the downside as compared to rates charged
business borrowers, the future is likely to see a change in this
pattern, reflecting three developments.

One is the likely strategy of major American financial institutions to focus more effort on domestic lending and investing, in
view of their past experience internationally. Second, household
lending offers an extraordinarily wide diversification of risks. It
should not be difficult to classify consumer borrowers by risk

category and charge differential interest rates based on relative risk, something that has been attempted only on a limited basis thus far. Third, and most important, profit margins in the consumer credit field will be squeezed by securitization similar to the securitization that has already taken place in mortgage lending.

The securitization of consumer credit, now just in its infancy, will be mature by 1995, with a variety of financial packages reaching the market. Some mutual funds, for example, will specialize in consumer-related securities; in view of the cash flow underlying consumer credit, these mutual funds will have quasi-money-market characteristics and thus induce some very short-term investors to lengthen their average maturities somewhat.

In another sector of household finance, mortgage borrowings, securitization has already taken hold and will be even larger a decade hence. For instance, the securitization of 1-to-4-family mortgages totaled 40 percent of new originations in 1985, up from 10 percent in 1975. This figure is likely to reach 70 percent by 1995.

In commercial property financing, securitization has begun and will be prominent by the middle of the next decade. Chances are also quite good that the securitization of both home and commercial mortgages will take place in other industrial nations, as their markets are deregulated and become more prominent as worldwide investment centers.

A related new entrant to securitization looms on the horizon —namely, equity values in real estate. This had an aborted beginning back in the seventies with the brief surge in the popularity of real estate investment trusts (REITs). However, many REITs lacked strong operating managements and thus performed poorly. Another effort to make large real estate values marketable is now underway. This was highlighted in 1985 by the sale of Rockefeller Center to the public for $1.3 billion.

If the securitization of equity values in real estate is to succeed, substantial progress will have to be made in establishing reliable quantitative methods to provide better reporting on real estate transactions, trading activity, investment performance, relative performance measurement, local and regional vacancy rates, occupancy turnover, and related matters. In addition, the standards and accuracy of real estate appraisals will have to be greatly improved. Even without a tradable real estate market, however, mortgages—the debt side of this market—will probably more than double by 1995, reaching perhaps $5 trillion in size as compared with $2.2 trillion at the end of 1985.

CHAPTER 17

The Changing Role of the Financial Economist

The performance of economists has come under scrutiny and criticism. This is not new, of course. Two centuries ago, Edmund Burke wrote, "The age of chivalry is gone. That of sophists, economists, and calculators has succeeded, and the glory of Europe is extinguished forever." Somewhat later Thomas Carlyle, in a similar vein, said, "Of all the quacks that ever quacked, political economists are the loudest. Instead of telling us what is meant by one's country, by what causes men are happy, moral, religious or the contrary, they tell us how flannel jackets are exchanged for pork hams. . . ."

Many economists agree—not with respect to their own work and their own ideas but with respect to the work and ideas of *other* economists. Debate within the ranks of economists is fierce, and economists speak unkind words about their own profession. One prominent economist has commented about the forecasting of cyclical trends by others that "reason, divination, incantation, and elements of witchcraft had been combined in a manner not elsewhere seen save in a primitive religion."

THE STATE OF ECONOMICS

Some of the criticism is justified and stems in part from the promise of accuracy that is being generated by the use of computers. Huge amounts of data can be massaged and reshaped by the computer. Econometric models proliferate and the results are carried to several decimal points, giving the illusory impression of extreme accuracy.

The quantification of statistical information has also contributed to economic ideas often being expressed in terms more appropriate for the exact physical sciences. Such terms as "soft landing" and "midcourse correction" may be appropriate for spaceships; however, they give misleading impressions with respect to economics because they imply that we can manipulate economic variables with a high degree of accuracy and precision. History continues to show that human behavior is highly complex and that the variables influencing it do not consistently produce predictable results. Keynes once expressed this succinctly by saying that human behavior is not "homogeneous through time."

Although economics and finance are often called "social sciences," what passes as "science" in the social area is far different from what is meant by that word in physics, chemistry, and related fields. There, the word "science" refers to a body of empirically testable propositions in which cause and effect are identifiable and can be objectively verified under controlled laboratory conditions. Since controlled laboratory experimentation and testing are virtually impossible in the social sciences—

217

in sociology, psychology, and economics, for example—they hardly qualify as sciences.

It was hoped that economics would come close to being a true science when mathematical models, sophisticated statistical techniques, and high-speed computers became integral parts of financial and economic analysis a decade or so ago. Simulations via econometric models were expected to approximate the controlled laboratory experiments of the physical sciences and produce more "scientific" conclusions. Unhappily, such hopes have not been realized, in part because econometric models are constructed on the basis of *past* statistical relationships. In times of rapid change, as has certainly been the case with the American financial system recently, past data provide poor guides to the future.

In addition, when multiple causation is involved, as is usually the case in the social sciences, mathematical-statistical techniques are rarely powerful enough to distinguish the relative strengths of various causes. "All other things" can be held constant in a laboratory more successfully than in the turbulent world of economics and finance.

The forecasting performance of economists has been under particularly close scrutiny. Whatever the overall record may be, it is probably no worse and perhaps better than in other fields of endeavor, where forecasts are not reported and publicized. Many business and financial decisions require implicit forecasts. How many wrong forecasts are made daily by securities traders, sales and production managers, or for that matter by senior business leaders or even heads of state?

Here are a few examples of wrong predictions made by people who have nevertheless left their imprint. After a disappointing flying experience in 1901, Wilbur Wright, brother of Orville, said, "Man won't fly for a thousand years." Thomas J. Watson, longtime head of IBM, said in 1958, "I think there is a world market for about five computers." Senator Daniel Webster said in 1848, "I cannot conceive of anything more ridiculous, more absurd, and more affrontive to sober judgment than the cry that we are profiting by the acquisition of New Mexico and California. I hold that they are not worth a dollar."

Still, economists have flourished. They continue to be hired by financial and nonfinancial firms at ever-rising salaries. Some have even become heads of states, others in charge of central banks or government treasuries. Many are involved in financial markets in one capacity or other, from senior management to staff technicians. Nevertheless, the economist's role is changing as financial markets change.

If economists are to remain useful and valuable, indeed if the profession is to grow in stature, several requirements will have to be fulfilled. First, more time and effort must be devoted to improving the accuracy of statistical data and to recognizing their shortcomings. Expressing statistical results in decimal points usually promotes misunderstanding of the precision that can be realized.

All too often, the precision is confined to the mathematical computations and sadly lacking in the validity of the data input. We have a strong tendency to accept statistical information as valid and then proceed to massage it in various ways to generate conclusions. But if the underlying data is only roughly accurate, or actually misleading, as has been known to be the case, all the sophisticated mathematical modeling in the world and carrying answers to three decimal points will not improve the accuracy of the conclusions.

Models have been rendered obsolete by statistical revisions. The revisions in the weekly and monthly money supply numbers are huge. The differences between the flash GNP, rendered before a quarter has ended, and the preliminary GNP, released a month later, are often large and further revisions are made subsequently. Models that seem to work well with one set of numbers often go completely awry with the revisions, leaving one to wonder what has gone wrong.

Second, statistics should not be used hastily as the basis for formulating theories, especially when the theories will be employed in deciding upon governmental stabilization policies. For example, the Phillips curve and the full employment budget are two theoretical concepts largely grounded in statistics that have not stood the test of time.

The Phillips curve posited a lasting relationship between the price level and the unemployment rate, based on some statistical relationships between the two that emerged from research conducted by British economist A. W. Phillips in the fifties. However, the relationships did not hold into the seventies, when unemployment rose but prices did not respond the way they were supposed to. With respect to the full employment budget, the definition of full employment has not remained constant: as a result of changing relationships between employment and prices, full employment, originally defined as about 4 percent unemployment, is currently considered to be around 6 percent.

A third prerequisite for furthering the functioning of economists in the future is to have better trained professionals who are willing to devote themselves to compiling, evaluating, and improving statistical data. The economics hierarchy does not assign a high status to those who spend their professional lives compiling or evaluating data. Indeed, the highest status levels are reserved for pure theorists who have nothing to do with statistical data in any form and probably wouldn't recognize data related to the real world if it hit them in the face. Everyone wants to erect models and spin theories, but hardly anyone wants to build the statistical foundations on which the models and theories must rest. The stature of those compiling and evaluating the quality of statistical series, and assessing their relevance, should be enhanced, and broader recognition should be given to those engaged in such work.

One hopes, too, economic and financial theory will soon emerge from its current impasse and once again be fruitful and productive. Economic theory has not been in such doldrums in over half a century—not since the early thirties, when classical economics found itself engulfed by the worldwide Great Depression and was unable to recommend any policies to end it besides laissez faire. To do nothing and let the economy take care of itself—laissez faire—was obviously not the appropriate medicine in 1932, with a fifth of the work force unemployed, the stock market in shambles, and much of American industry shut down, but economic theory could come up with nothing else until John Maynard Keynes rationalized fiscal intervention in *The General Theory of Employment, Interest and Money* (1936).

After World War II, Keynesian economics dominated the profession for about a quarter century. By showing how depression and recession could be ameliorated by public policy, Keynesian economics gained esteem and blossomed in the fifties and sixties. Economists in general were considered *useful,* and were respected far more in government and in business than they had been previously. In finance, the development of the flow of funds accounts in the fifties and sixties complemented Keynesian economics and helped economists get involved in the securities markets and the financial services industry generally.

Keynesians contributed to their own downfall by promising more than they could deliver. The early-sixties view that fiscal policy could successfully "fine-tune" the economy to any degree desired helped discredit Keynesian theory by building up expectations to an unrealistic level.

Even more important in the downfall of Keynesian economics, however, was the onset of double-digit inflation and the inability of Keynesian theory to prescribe a workable remedy. Keynesian theory came to prominence on its real-world ability to stop depression, but it fell from grace because it had no similar practical remedy for inflation. In large part *because* of Keynes, the persistent postwar problem has not been depression but inflation, for which Keynesian theory has no workable remedies. The double-digit inflation of the seventies and early eighties thus paved the way for the decline of Keynesianism and the rise of monetarism.

Monetarism has a practical program to combat inflation—control the money supply—just as Keynesian economics in the thirties had a practical program to combat depression—deficit spending. Both have their costs, however. Keynesian prescriptions are quite effective in stopping recession, but in the environment of the eighties they risk promoting inflation. On the other hand, monetarist prescriptions are quite effective in stopping inflation, but they invite unemployment and recession. Just as Keynesian theory has trouble handling inflation, monetarism has similar trouble handling unemployment and recession. In effect, monetarism reverts to classical economics and laissez faire by recommending that nothing be done to ameliorate recession, that it be left alone to cure itself.

We are thus at an impasse in the eighties, with both Keynesian and monetarist economics under a cloud. Neither appears capable of handling the complex problems of the last decade and a half of the twentieth century. We need an economic theory that is appropriate for the present era, one more in tune with our complex and internationally oriented economy.

Such a theory should include an improved analysis of economic and financial linkages within a worldwide framework. Neither Keynesian nor monetarist theory adequately addresses the interactions of financial and economic variables in the economy. Indeed, monetarists virtually ignore such matters in their concentration on the money supply to the virtual exclusion of credit flows. Keynesian theory is compatible with the incorporation of credit flows, although it has tended to emphasize stocks in its financial sectors rather than flows. And neither Keynesianism nor monetarism takes adequate account of the international repercussions of policies. Both are essentially domestic in their orientation. This might have been acceptable in the past, but it will not do in the present or for the future.

WORK OF THE FINANCIAL ECONOMIST

The work of the financial economist in the nineties is not likely to involve the heavy load of near-term, week-to-week, and month-to-month projections that presently occupy a large share of his (or her) time. Much of what is done by hand today should soon be computerized and displayed on information screens at the touch of a button: such as projections of the index of industrial production, personal income, housing starts, retail sales, inflation indices, and leading economic indicators. Junior rather than senior analysts will be able to track such variables and report to someone higher up the line when anything develops that appears worth more intensive examination. Similarly, projections of Federal Reserve operations and of money supply (if such a concept is still valid a decade hence) will require only routine attention then, unlike the army of well-paid Fed watchers who now examine every move of the central bank for clues regarding its intentions.

But another part of the financial economist's job is likely to increase in importance—namely, mathematical calculations of financial asset and liability value relationships, work that is already well underway at many firms. Investigation is likely to be particularly intense into analysis of hedging and arbitrage involving many securities and on the specifics of determining mortgage yields. If the real estate market becomes securitized, as I expect it will, much of the basic groundwork regarding technical details and yield calculations will be laid by financial analysts and economists.

Many other similar areas will also occupy a large share of attention. Relationships integrating interest rates and currency values in major financial centers around the world will be greatly refined and of more use to traders and investors. Many of the new proxy credit instruments that are proliferating here and abroad will require attention by analysts and economists. Financial economists will make major contributions to building a huge matrix of investment and trading alternatives and opportunities, encompassing hundreds of domestic and international securities, that will show various risk and reward combinations involved in shifting from one to another or to multiples of other obligations. To properly utilize such tools, the trader of the future will require a strong analytic background, or ready access to someone with such knowledge, suggesting that more economists may land at or near trading desks and be actively involved in the trading process.

While much near-term forecasting will be highly mechanical if not entirely computerized, the financial economist will not be able to escape responsibility for intermediate and longer-term forecasting, with judgment coming into play frequently in the exercise of such forecasting. This means predicting cyclical turning points in the economy, anticipating structural changes in financial and business markets and in financial institutions, and alerting coworkers to the implications of such changes, as well as forecasting the directions of change in interest rates.

These are demanding responsibilities. No two business or financial cycles have ever been exactly alike. Surprises in the macro economy are standard fare. Structural changes are difficult to discern; they are never contained in "consensus" estimates compiled by combining the estimates of many economists. Large econometric models build in such basic changes only well after the fact.

THREE FORECASTS IN RETROSPECT

In my own financial forecasting, I have always found that a reasonably accurate economic forecast is necessary but not sufficient in arriving at a financial forecast (that is, a forecast of interest rates and perhaps stock prices). Let me illustrate by three examples from the past dealing with the forecasting of cyclical interest rate peaks and troughs: (1) the peak in 1974, (2) the trough in 1977, and (3) the peak in 1981.

The Peak in 1974

I was fortunate enough to correctly call the cyclical downturn in interest rates that began in October 1974 following a sharp and longer-than-generally-expected rise in rates. This cyclical interest-rate rise, which began in 1971 and endured for about three years, had many unusual characteristics.

By the time it was over, long-term rates had moved to new postwar highs. Long-term AA utility bonds rose from 6.9 percent at their cyclical low to 10.6 percent at their cyclical high. Lower quality bond yields continued to move up well after the cyclical peak was reached on higher quality bonds.

An important ingredient was that the Franklin National Bank encountered irreversible financial difficulty and was officially declared insolvent on October 8, 1974, by the Comptroller of the Currency and the Federal Deposit Insurance Corporation. With over $2 billion in deposits a few months earlier, Franklin National was at the time the largest bank failure in U.S. history. The institution was taken over by the European-American Bank, which is owned by a consortium of six large European banks.

The President of the United States, Richard M. Nixon, also resigned that summer (on August 9, 1974), and was succeeded by Vice President Gerald R. Ford.

From an interest-rate-forecasting viewpoint, a key dilemma was the rise in rates well into the economic recession that started in November 1973, a full eleven months before long-term interest rates reached their cyclical peak.

The reasons I correctly waited until well into the recession to call the cyclical peak were contained in a talk I gave to the Securities Industry Association in September 1973:

> In assessing money and bond market prospects, it is very helpful to distinguish clearly between the policies of monetary restraint in 1969–70 and those of 1973 and the respective roles of commercial banks and business corpora-

225

tions in the two periods. Monetary restraint in the 1969–70 period was designed to limit the availability of new money through the general market process which involved, in addition to rising interest rates, an emphasis on various "frictional" devices. The frictional devices were the Regulation Q ceilings on both savings deposits and negotiable CDs, pressure on banks to halt the rise in the prime loan rate when it reached 8½ percent, and the legal interest rate ceilings that inhibited other borrowers. The main consequences of this strategy were a sharp curtailment of the inflow of new funds to deposit-type institutions including commercial banks and life insurance companies. Disintermediation occurred quickly and at a lower level of interest rates at that time than in the current period of restraint.

Now, the new monetary strategy is to slow the availability of new funds in the marketplace with many of the earlier frictional devices removed. Regulation Q has been liberalized. There is now a modified floating prime loan rate and the interest-rate ceiling on the financing of private homes has been raised. Furthermore, reserve requirements on Eurodollar borrowings were aligned with those on negotiable CDs. Therefore, the price of money largely determines who will be the ultimate recipient of the funds.

In the current round of monetary restraint the commercial banks, rather than having to experience the impact of disintermediation, have become a vehicle of competitive intermediation. The ultimate significance of this new strategy is unknown. It forces the commercial banking system to be aggressive bidders for funds to meet enlarged demands.

The Trough in 1977

In a subsequent cyclical rally, I waited well into the economic recovery before I anticipated the trough in 1977. Then in late

September 1976, I wrote a special memorandum to portfolio managers:

> We are now very near or perhaps even at the cyclical low for high-grade long-term interest rates. Short-term interest rates probably reached their lows last spring. This is not to say that a pronounced new upswing in interest rates is imminent. A meaningful lift in short-term interest rates will most likely not get underway until sometime in 1977 and long-term rates should be in a trendless sort of trading range for some time.

Long-term interest rates actually bottomed out in January 1977, 28 months after they had started in a downward direction. The decline in rates (rise in bond prices) persisted so long because of an extraordinary effort by business and households to recoup liquidity. Business corporations actually had a contraction in capital outlays in the first year following the trough in business activity, and borrowed long-term aggressively to pay off short-term debt. However, by the fourth quarter of 1976, business corporations had gone a long way toward improving their financial well-being.

State and local governments, which were substantially inhibited by the credit stringencies of 1974, as well as by the financial deterioration of some major cities, had returned to the municipal bond market to issue a huge volume of long-term debt. Financial institutions had also made important progress in improving their liquidity. The decline in interest rates by the fall of 1976 was of average cyclical proportions. Another manifestation of the lessening of financial tensions was the sharp narrowing of the yield spread between high- and medium-quality issues; as medium-quality borrowers improved their financial positions, they required less of a rate differential above high-quality borrowers to sell their securities.

227

The Financial Future

The Peak in 1981

Thereafter began the most dramatic cyclical rise in interest rates that we have yet experienced. From the cyclical low of 1976–77 to the next peak in 1981, yields on 3-month Treasury bills rose from 4¼ percent to 17¼ percent and long-term Governments from about 7¼ percent to 15¼ percent. The upswing was briefly but dramatically interrupted by a rally in bond prices in the spring of 1980, when President Jimmy Carter imposed some selective consumer credit controls for a few months.

I stayed bearish (anticipating lower bond prices, higher interest rates) throughout this period, except for the brief interlude in the spring of 1980. I turned bullish (higher bond prices, lower interest rates) belatedly in the summer of 1982. My views were influenced by a number of differences in the environment at that time compared with the past.

One difference was the intransigence of inflation, which rose to double-digit rates and did not quickly abate with the slowing-down of the economy. A second important difference from earlier economic periods was the international petroleum constraint, which contributed to inflationary pressures. Third, the performance of the dollar in world foreign exchange markets was weak, whereas previously it had been strong; a combination of developments—the capital transfers due to oil, which was mainly priced in dollars, and the high inflation rate in the United States—made the dollar quite vulnerable. A fourth difference was the adoption of monetarism as a guiding principle by the Federal Reserve and a much tighter and more rigid monetary policy than we had previously experienced.

A fifth important difference from the past that encouraged me to stay bearish was the rapid growth of arbitraging by all types of financial institutions and participants. Institutions increasingly were eliminating interest-rate risk from their lending through such credit instruments as the floating prime rate, variable interest-rate mortgages, and floating-rate CDs and notes. It seemed to me at the time that interest-rate levels were no longer the powerful regulators of economic activity that they had been.

Finally, I sensed that fiscal policy did not and would not have the flexibility that advocates of fiscal policy had promised and hoped for.

My belated but much heralded turn to a bullish interest-rate outlook on August 17, 1982, which helped trigger one of the largest price gains in bonds and stocks in modern times, was mainly influenced by my belief that a vigorous economic rebound was not in the offing, that major financial institutions were not in any position to implement aggressive lending and investing programs quickly, and that the international debt overhang would restrict borrowers as well as lenders. Of course, if I had sensed these restrictive influences and their retarding influence earlier, I would have turned bullish earlier. In forecasting, there is no mechanical technique for achieving perfection. Forecasting is an art, not a science, and judgment remains paramount.

In the future, financial economists and analysts will find forecasting increasingly difficult. Finding similarities with the past will often provide little comfort, although they should not be ignored. But in a world of financial innovation, deregulation, close linkages of markets domestically and internationally, and instantaneous communication, spotting fundamental and structural *differences* from the past will probably provide better clues to accurate analysis and forecasting.

Financial economists and analysts will be in a unique position to make contributions to business profitability and to economic progress in the next decade. The proliferation of credit instruments, financing techniques, and vast matrices of trading and investing opportunities requires highly objective evaluations of risks and rewards, and a sense of historical perspective, if excessive risk taking is to be voided.

To make this objectivity effective, however, will often require convincing others to give up the pursuit of high but uncertain short-term rewards in order to settle for lower but more certain long-term compensation. This means withstanding numerous and powerful pressures from time to time, combined with a willingness to persist and persevere even though one may be outside the general consensus.

PART V

Epilogue

CHAPTER 18

Judging Economic and Financial Performance

I think it is appropriate to close with some observations of a more general and speculative nature. In that vein, one of our most popular pastimes is the making of judgments assessing performance. Its proliferation, from sports to economics, is mainly the result of vast improvements in technology, communications, and in techniques of interpretation. Not only are there legions of people now in the business of collecting statistics about virtually everything under the sun, but an enormous computer capability is available to store and rearrange historical information and it can be programmed to project data in a nearly endless variety of ways.

Indeed, looking at data in terms of such statistical procedures as "average," "median," or "standard deviation" is old hat. The sophisticated analysts of today have a whole new language that only a few understand. They explain business and financial activities in terms of exponential smoothing, autocorrelation, covariance matrices, and Box-Jenkins techniques. At the same time, business statistics have become hot news items for the press, thereby increasing the pressure to turn every weekly and monthly indicator virtually inside out in order to rapidly spot possible changes in trends.

The improved techniques for measuring performance have contributed importantly to the conduct of business and finance. It is hard to imagine how our forefathers could have succeeded without computers, calculators, Scantlin machines, and other rapid information-transmitting devices. But even with our modern-day wizardry, we still face shortcomings in making judgments.

OBJECTIVES

The current plethora of instant interpretations tends to emphasize the near-term without adequate regard for longer-term objectives. The problem is compounded by the compressed time scales within which business and government function.

Judgments on the performance of our economy require a clearly defined objective. Too often, the objective is taken for granted, or there are multiple and contradictory objectives. Unless we are clear on our objective or objectives, we are not able to evaluate performance as good or bad or somewhere in between.

A list of national economic objectives might include optimum growth, full employment, price stability, accumulation of wealth, greater equality of income distribution, increased productivity, racial equality, improved health and environment, and balance in international payments. Some of these are precisely measurable while others are not, even though they may be just as important. To achieve some, others may have to be compromised.

The time element is particularly vexing. Serious assessments can hardly be made on the basis of events spanning a week or a month. But in many cases calendar or fiscal years or political terms in office hardly provide an adequate framework either. When business and political leaders assume their roles, they undertake them in the midst of complex ongoing activities. Often the real value of management decisions does not become apparent until many years later.

Perhaps what we should do is try to analyze the impact of decisions in any one period on longer-term performance. In the political arena, for example, why should we emphasize the skill and acumen of national policy-makers only on the basis of the new initiatives they introduce and legislate? Sometimes the events that do *not* materialize are more important than those that do. We should try to ascertain what decisions political leaders are undertaking that will benefit their nations *subsequent* to their terms in office.

The time element also involves fashions in economic judgments. Those who lived prior to the 1929 crash thought they were in a new era without real risks. As the crash and subsequent events took their toll, theories of economic maturity and stagnation became popular and the views of John Maynard Keynes dominated the classrooms and the boardrooms. These were not challenged until inflation eclipsed unemployment as our major economic concern. Monetarism, led by Professor Milton Friedman, thereupon fashionably superseded Keynesian ideas in many quarters.

Similarly, in the years right after World War II the prevailing opinion was that 2½ percent interest rates on long-term U.S. Government bonds would last forever and that common stocks had limited investment value. Twenty years later, near the end of the sixties, one financial magazine forecast that bonds would follow dinosaurs into extinction while stocks, it said, would dominate investor portfolios. Not so long ago, portfolio managers prided themselves on the individuality of their investment selections. Now it is the vogue to invest in securities that reflect broadly based indices because, it is believed, no one can consistently outperform the market.

LONG-TERM TRENDS

In making economic judgments, we are also inclined to look for comparability and similarity of events. Seasonality and cyclicality are stressed, while longer-lasting forces are minimized. Just as accountants compartmentalize the financial and operational life of a business, economists do the same with the pattern of business activity. While this approach often provides useful insights, it simultaneously oversimplifies the complexities of economic life and sometimes obscures important ongoing activities.

Of course, economic judgments about the future are heavily influenced by the current situation and the immediate past. Very often the future is interpreted as an extension of the recent past. When conditions are good, the tendency is to conclude they will get better, and vice versa. This approach may sometimes work for projecting nearer-term trends, but surprise-free scenarios do not contain the elements of change that influence the longer term.

To illustrate the problem of perceiving fundamental or longer-lasting change, I want to examine a few pages from history and ask whether a reasonable person, armed with today's analytical skills, could have been expected to foresee the changes that took place.

At the dawn of history, life was dominated by huge dinosaurs, fifty-foot crocodiles, and the seas swarmed with twenty-foot lizards. The mammals, small and shrewlike in form, hid in the thickets and grasses during the day and ventured out only at twilight or in the dark. Undoubtedly, a modern-day rating agency would have accorded the dinosaurs the highest credit rating and given no rating at all to the frightened mammals. Today, the dinosaurs are extinct and mammals are the dominant life form.

How many living in biblical times were able to perceive the far-reaching impact that deliverance of the Ten Commandments would have on the morality and behavior standards of much of mankind?

Perhaps these two illustrations are too remote. More recently, therefore, how many would have made a correct judgment about the rise of the United States to world leadership had they lived in the nineteenth century? Textbooks often describe the United States of the nineteenth century as a succession of excesses and calamities. The economy is pictured in terms of wild speculation, knavery, and irresponsible finance. There was the crisis of 1837, the panic of 1857, the dislocations of the Civil War, the panic of 1873, and the financial panics of 1884 and 1893. During these periods of travail, securities prices fell sharply and banks suspended specie payments. In one panic, fourteen railroads went into bankruptcy, and in another, six hundred banks failed. Nevertheless, it was during this century that the West was settled and developed, massive railroad construction took place, prosperity was occasionally spectacular, and the United States began to blossom into an industrial giant.

Consider how hard it would have been to project some of the major developments around the world if in 1945 one were standing in the ruins of World War II. How predictable was the spectacular recovery staged by Germany and Japan? Or the rapid growth of multinational corporations and the development of international financial networks?

There is simply no scientific procedure that yields accurate economic judgments about the long term. Even so, a few observations might be helpful:

Epilogue

First, history shows that to project the future by merely extending the past is a dangerous thing. In this century alone, each decade has differed sharply from its predecessor. The decade of the 1910s was marked by World War I; the twenties by speculation; the thirties by worldwide depression; the forties by World War II; the fifties by economic recovery and rehabilitation; the sixties by a long economic expansion and sowing the seeds of inflation; the seventies by oil shortages and double-digit inflation; and the eighties, so far, by disinflation and deregulation.

Second, fashions in economic judgments are dangerous. They contribute to unsustainable business momentum, either up or down.

Third, leadership—be it in business, finance, industry, or culture—has a definite life cycle. The duration of this life cycle varies. We need only look to the Roman Empire, ancient Greece, and Spain for examples. In the business world, IBM was an unknown when the American railroads were the elite credit in the marketplace.

Fourth, finance is the handmaiden of economic growth. It serves as both the stick and the carrot, encouraging growth with new funds and disciplining those who have abused contractual relationships. Developments in finance tend to reflect the strengths and weaknesses of mankind.

Fifth, the interdependence of nations will in all probability tend to increase with further rapid strides in science and technology.

Sixth, in a world marked by substantial differences between the industrial and less-developed nations, between rich and poor, between educated and illiterate, between countries having deep-seated ideological differences, in a world wherein nuclear warfare is an ever-present danger, limits to economic growth based on past and present productive technology are not an acceptable solution. Nor is the shortsighted neglect of future economic potential.

If the world is to survive, objectives and efforts simply *must* be directed to the enlargement of production and wealth throughout the globe in order to provide outlets for human achievement and to raise living standards worldwide.

Suggestions for Further Reading

Inquiries into the background of and conditions leading to financial crises have attracted considerable attention in recent years. I would particularly recommend Albert M. Wojnilower's brilliant study "The Central Role of Credit Crunches in Recent Financial History," in *Brookings Papers on Economic Activity*, Number 2 (1980); *Crises in the Economic and Financial Structure*, edited by Paul Wachtel (Lexington Books: Salomon Brothers Center for the Study of Financial Institutions, New York University, 1982); and *Financial Crises: Institutions and Markets in a Fragile Environment*, edited by Edward I. Altman and Arnold W. Sametz (John Wiley and Sons: Salomon Brothers Center for the Study of Financial Institutions, New York University, 1977).

Financial markets and institutions have been changing so dramatically in recent years that books tend to get rapidly out of date. However, Elbert V. Bowden and Judith L. Holbert's *Revolution in Banking*, 2nd edition (Englewood Cliffs, N.J.: Prentice-Hall, 1984), and Martin Mayer's *The Money Bazaars* (New York: E. P. Dutton, 1984), are two volumes that continue to reward the reader with fresh insights regarding what has been happening in financial markets and institutions and why. Anthony Sampson's *The Money Lenders* (New York: Viking Press, 1981), a well-received inquiry into some of the international aspects of finance, complements the Bowden-Holbert and Mayer books.

It is also instructive, in terms of the changes that have been taking place in the banking industry, to compare Mayer's *The Money Bazaars*, published in 1984, with his earlier well-known book, *The Bankers*, published by Weybright and Talley back in 1974, when the financial waters were still relatively calm. For a useful summary of the structure of banking systems worldwide, see Vicente Muro, *World Banking Handbook* (Los Angeles, Cal.: Business Guides, 1984).

The implications of financial deregulation are analyzed and discussed in *The Deregulation of the Banking and Securities Industries*, edited by Lawrence G. Goldberg and Lawrence J. White (Lexington Books: Salomon Brothers Center for the Study of Financial Institutions, New York University, 1979); in *Securities Activities of Commercial Banks*, edited by Arnold W. Sametz (Lexington Books: Salomon Brothers Center for the Study of Financial Institutions, New York University, 1983); and in *The Emerging Financial Industry*, edited by Arnold W. Sametz (Lexington Books: Salomon Brothers Center for the Study of Financial Institutions, New York University, 1983).

For details on the functioning of the bond and stock markets, two standard sources are David M. Darst's *The Complete Bond Book* (New York: McGraw-Hill, 1975) and Burton G. Malkiel's *A Random Walk Down Wall Street,* 4th edition (New York: W. W. Norton, 1985). State and local bonds are discussed by Robert Lamb and Stephen Rappaport in their excellent *Municipal Bonds* (New York: McGraw-Hill, 1980). For developments in futures and options, see Mark Powers and David Vogel, *Inside the Financial Futures Markets,* 2nd edition (New York: John Wiley, 1984).

The money market and its institutions and practices are fully analyzed in Marcia Stigum, *The Money Market,* revised edition (Homewood, Ill.: Dow Jones-Irwin, 1983). Two other useful sources in this area are *Instruments of the Money Market,* published by the Federal Reserve Bank of Richmond in 1981; and Gunter Dufey and Ian H. Giddy, *The International Money Market* (Englewood Cliffs, N.J.: Prentice-Hall, 1978). A considerable amount of interesting material is also in Paul Meek's *U.S. Monetary Policy and Financial Markets* (Federal Reserve Bank of New York, 1982). Mr. Meek held the position of Monetary Adviser at the New York Fed. This volume is the successor to a small book that attracted quite a bit of attention when it was published by the Federal Reserve Bank of New York in 1956, namely Robert V. Roosa's *Federal Reserve Operations in the Money and Government Securities Markets.* Roosa's book was the first thorough exposition of how the Federal Reserve conducted its open-market operations. Finally with respect to the money market, even though it was written more than a decade ago, Wesley Lindow's *Inside the Money Market* (New York: Random House, 1972) still reads well today.

Historical data on rates of return yielded by alternative investments are contained in Roger G. Ibbotson and Rex A. Sinquefield's *Stocks, Bonds, Bills, and Inflation: The Past and the Future* (Charlottesville, Va.: Financial Analysts Research Foundation, 1982). Similar data are extended to gold and residential housing by Lawrence S. Ritter and Thomas J. Urich in *The Role of Gold in Consumer Investment Portfolios* (New York University: Salomon Brothers Center for the Study of Financial Institutions, 1984). See also James H. Lorie, Peter Dodd, and Mary Hamilton Kimpton, *The Stock Market: Theories and Evidence*, 2nd edition (Homewood, Ill.: Richard D. Irwin, 1985); and *Paul Erdman's Money Book: An Investor's Guide to Economics and Finance* (New York: Random House, 1984).

Technological developments in the payments system and the financial services industry are discussed in *The Future of the U.S. Payments System* (Federal Reserve Bank of Atlanta, 1981); and in *Report on the Payments System* (Washington, D.C.: Association of Reserve City Bankers, 1982). Although not so up to date, there is still a lot of interesting material in Mark J. Flannery and Dwight M. Jaffee's, *The Economic Implications of an Electronic Monetary Transfer System* (Lexington, Mass.: Lexington Books, 1973), and in *Financial Innovation*, edited by William L. Silber (Lexington Books: Salomon Brothers Center for the Study of Financial Institutions, New York University, 1975).

With respect to interest rates, I can recommend nothing more valuable than Sidney Homer's justly famous *A History of Interest Rates*, revised edition (New Brunswick, N.J.: Rutgers University Press, 1975). Closely related, for technicians, is Sidney Homer and Martin L. Liebowitz's pioneering *Inside the Yield Book* (Englewood Cliffs, N.J.: Prentice-Hall, 1972). A good survey of many interest-rate issues will be found in James C. Van Horne's *Financial Market Rates and Flows* (Englewood Cliffs, N.J.: Prentice-Hall, 1978).

Anyone who wants to know more about monetarism and its implications for monetary policy-making is well advised to consult the experts directly: long before Milton Friedman arrived on the scene, there was Irving Fisher with *The Purchasing Power of Money* (New York: Macmillan, 1911), which expounded in great detail the quantity theory of money, forerunner of today's monetarist philosophy. Professor Friedman's views on monetarism are contained in his *A Program for Monetary Stability* (New

York: Fordham University Press, 1959); and also in Milton Friedman and Anna J. Schwartz's *A Monetary History of the United States* (Princeton, N.J.: Princeton University Press, 1963).

Opinions that disagree with Professor Friedman are expressed by Marriner Eccles in his autobiography, *Beckoning Frontiers* (New York: Alfred A. Knopf, 1951); by Allan Sproul in *The Selected Papers of Allan Sproul* (Federal Reserve Bank of New York, 1980); and of course by John Maynard Keynes in his classic *The General Theory of Employment, Interest, and Money* (New York: Harcourt Brace, 1936). Marriner Eccles was chairman of the Federal Reserve Board from 1934 to 1948 and Allan Sproul was president of the Federal Reserve Bank of New York from 1941 to 1956. An up-to-date assessment of the relevance of Keynes's ideas in the present-day environment can be found in *Keynes and the Modern World,* proceedings of a conference held on the one hundredth anniversary of Keynes's birth (Cambridge, England: Cambridge University Press, 1983).

Several "handbooks" that contain a number of articles on specialized subjects, authored by experts, are worth consulting when understanding in depth is sought on specific topics. In this category are *The Real Estate Handbook,* edited by Maury Seldin; *The Handbook of Fixed Income Securities,* edited by Frank J. Fabozzi and Irving M. Pollack; *The Handbook of Financial Markets: Securities, Options, and Futures,* edited by Frank J. Fabozzi and Frank G. Zarb; and *The Investment Manager's Handbook,* edited by Sumner N. Levine. All are published in Homewood, Illinois, by Dow Jones-Irwin. A collection of some of the best articles from all the handbooks has been issued under the title *Readings in Investment Management,* edited by Frank J. Fabozzi (Homewood, Ill.: Richard D. Irwin, 1983).

Index